Contents

To Mum & Dad &
my Delicious Derek

Acknowledgements

Writing this book has been a great adventure but like all adventures, it was only possible with lots of help along the way.

Firstly, my thanks to Dominic, Patrick and the ladies at Mercier Press for thinking this book was a good idea and for their absolute professionalism at all times. It has been a pleasure to work with such a wonderful team.

My close friends have supported me on my Delicious journey and this project was no exception as they helped me with recipes, ideas and suggestions along the way.

To my mum, Mary, and sister, Louise, for all for their help on recipes and baking, and to Lizette, for help all the way from New Zealand.

For Dad, my coeliac and avid supporter; whether it's for sampling cakes or helping to bake them, I would not be here without his patience and support.

For Derek, my husband, who offers good humour, clever ideas and endless support, whilst also being a great baker!

My thanks to Claire O'Donovan, our marketing student who spent months deciphering my scribbled recipes. Also, my thanks to Michael Mealy of The Kitchen Centre, Douglas, for the use of his beautiful kitchens for our photo shoot, and to Ray O'Leary of Premier Catering for providing us with equipment to make everything run smoothly. Finally, to the Delicious team for all their work and in particular to Connie for a loan of her mum's gingerbread recipe!

Introduction

Welcome to Denise's Delicious gluten-free baking. When I was invited by Mercier Press to write this book it gave me a welcome and long overdue chance to compile years of recipes, baking secrets and tips, family stories and anecdotes from my bakery that have come together to chart the story of my own experience of gluten-free baking. I am delighted to have the opportunity to share my experience with readers who, for whatever reason, also have a particular interest in gluten-free baking.

For me, baking for family and friends is very much a part of who I am. As a passionate home-baker, baking and family times just go naturally together. At home a family occasion was not a real get together unless we had cake, plenty of it, and, of course, it had to be home-baked.

I was lucky to come from a family where Mum, a fully committed home-baker, cherished the tradition of baking for her family using the tried and trusted master recipe book that had been handed down to her by her mother, who had it from her mother before her. Every generation of the family has left its own imprint on our home-baking bible and writing this book now brings yet another new and much larger chapter to the family's baking history, as I have become the gluten-free baker of the family.

From as far back as I can remember, I loved to bake. But my interest in baking took an unexpected turn when Dad was diagnosed with coeliac disease and needed to adapt to a gluten-free diet. As my father made his journey into the new and unknown world of gluten-free, I decided that he could do with a supportive companion.

As you will see from some of the recounted highlights of the journey we took, little did I know what lay ahead for us gluten-free pioneers!

Post Dad's diagnosis, and after much trial and error, we were able to successfully bake for him at home and he gradually began to enjoy once more the delicious home baking that we had all just taken for granted previous to his diagnosis. The fact that he could indeed have his gluten-free cake and eat it marked the start of our exploration of a gluten-free diet that was both delicious and safe for him to enjoy, but that could also be offered to any other coeliacs. What began as a home-baking effort to cater for his own needs, prompted Dad and me to research the possibility of founding our own gluten-free bakery.

After years of juggling training to be a specialist baker with living in London where I worked as an investment banker, it was time to go solo and to pursue my heart's desire: I set up my own gluten-free bakery. Denise's Delicious Gluten Free Bakery, Ireland's first artisan gluten-free bakery, had arrived.

I am writing this introduction at a time when the gluten-free market is really beginning to blossom in Ireland and, as a pioneer in the field, Delicious is delighted to be joined by an increasing number of newcomers to the arena. As Ireland's longest established artisan gluten-free bakery, we at Delicious have witnessed first-hand the baking challenges for the dad in his forties who has never had a birthday cake or for the busy mum struggling with the reality of cooking Christmas dinner in a gluten-free way for a ten-year-old just diagnosed with coeliac disease. Helping these 'free-from friends' gives us great job satisfaction and thankfully the choices available for those following a free-from diet have increased enormously. It is so wonderful to see customers now choosing to follow a gluten-free lifestyle because it makes them feel better.

My fundamental belief in the importance of using natural ingredients lies at the heart of my own and the Delicious gluten-free philosophy, as you will see from the ingredients lists featured in this publication.

My understanding of what makes not just good, but great flavour was shaped during my years of working for an Italian bank. My Italian co-workers, whilst bankers, were all very knowledgeable about food. They really helped me understand ingredients and how to combine flavours well whilst all the time keeping things simple. The simplicity of the recipes throughout this book is the result of years of painstaking work that took place literally over a hot stove!

My belief, when we first opened the door of the bakery, still rings true today: if you are following a restricted diet that does not have to mean a compromised food choice or experience. I think life should not be spent having unsatisfying food experiences, no matter what eating choices we may choose or have to follow. This book unveils a new departure in the bakery's story as we aim to help the home-baker who struggles to find good recipes that they know will work every time. Bakers who use this book will develop an understanding of the different ingredients in the world of gluten-free and be guided on what ingredients marry well.

Gluten-free baking is tricky if you don't have a road map. You'll be glad to know that these recipes work; just follow the steps and take it slowly.

This book is a salute to all of my customers who love my recipes and like to bake them at home. You have supported me and joined me along the gluten-free journey and for that I am touched and grateful. Long may we continue on our journey together. And remember, always bake with joy!

Denise's Gluten-free Baking Tips

The following list of tips should help you in baking, whether it is gluten-free or not.

Bain marie for melting chocolate: Chocolate is a difficult ingredient to work with and, in particular when you need to melt it, it can misbehave. A good tip for melting chocolate is to create a bain marie: heat water in a saucepan and find a bowl that is sturdy (not plastic) that sits snugly into the saucepan, but doesn't touch the water. Put your chocolate into the bowl and it will melt from the heat of the water without being in direct contact with the heat source.

Baking beans: When baking 'regular' pastry cases blind (i.e. without a filling) you need to have baking beans on the pastry to weigh it down in the oven, so that the pastry does not puff up during baking time. For gluten-free baking this is not the case, as the pastry does not puff up at all. It is an easier life to bake gluten-free!

Baking powder: Do tread carefully with baking powder, as it is often one of those ingredients that you expect to be gluten-free, when in fact most do contain some wheat flour. Make sure to buy a good quality, certified gluten-free (GF) brand.

Cider vinegar: This is a wonderful ingredient with enormous health benefits. One of its uses is that it acts as a natural preservative for bread, so consider adding one teaspoon to your recipe.

Cocoa powder: Cocoa powder is very fine and difficult to blend with flour as it often clumps. The best solution is to sieve it with your flour three times. This will ensure it is fully mixed in with the flour and you will avoid streaks in your cakes.

Conversions: Please stick to either the metric or imperial measurements when using these recipes as conversions are not exact, but will work if used consistently.

Custard/Curds: A skin will form naturally on a custard or curd as it cools. If this is then mixed into the custard, it is unpleasant. Make sure to place a piece of greaseproof paper on the surface while it is still warm. When you are ready to use the custard, peel off the greaseproof paper and the skin will peel away with it, leaving the cooled custard ready to use.

Curdling: A simple step which is often overlooked. To prevent a sauce or curd from curdling, always add a little of the hot liquid to the cold ingredients and mix together. Then add this to the remaining hot liquid. It will prevent curdling and the lumps that occur if you add the cold ingredients straight into the hot.

Dairy-free baking: This book is intended as a gluten- and wheat-free recipe book. However, I have stated in each recipe that you can use butter or margarine. If you are baking dairy-free, then use a dairy-free baking margarine, which should be easy to find. The recipes will work perfectly. For the fillings where I use fresh cream or cheese it is possible to substitute a dairy-free cream or cheese. Alternatively, you can use a buttercream made with a dairy-free margarine as filling for the sponges.

Fast-track caramel: Our Millionaire's Shortbread recipe involves making caramel. This means standing over a pot and stirring vigorously for quite a while. Now, while this does make the most wonderful caramel, you may not always have time for it. A tip is to buy tins of condensed milk, place them in a large pot of water, bring to the boil and boil for about 2 hours and then allow to cool. The milk will turn into a soft caramel. Great to have in the cupboard and you'll never be stuck for an impromptu dessert. I've never had a tin explode on me, but I suppose there are no guarantees on that front! The important thing is to ensure the tins are completely covered by the water at all times.

Gluten-free flours: This is really the most complex part of gluten-free baking and I could write a book on gluten-free flours alone. The key is to understand your recipes and keep practising. To make matters easier, I have included a recipe for my flour blend, which will work for all the recipes in this book unless something else is specified, but is also a great cupboard staple for your everyday baking. I would make a kilo of it, pop it in a Tupperware container and then you have it to hand. Some of my recipes contain other flours, so here is a brief summary of the most common gluten-free flour types, in case you choose to experiment. I think it is important to use a combination of flours because no one flour can really stand alone.

1. *Buckwheat Flour:* A flour that has been in use for a long time and is traditionally used for galettes (savoury crêpes) in Brittany. Brown in colour and very versatile. I find it to be somewhat coarse, so when baked it can result in grittiness.

2. *Carob Flour:* This is an extract from the carob bean. It's brown in colour and is often used as a substitute for chocolate. I like to use it in brown flour for colour and texture, and in a combination with other flours, rather than on its own.

3. *Chestnut Flour:* Obviously derived from chestnuts. I don't use this a lot because of nut allergies. It is a heavy flour and is brown in colour. Lovely for heavy recipes, such as tortes or

fudgy brownies. I would shy away from using it for a sponge or pastry.

4. *Corn Flour:* This is very common in gluten-free baking but some individuals cannot tolerate corn, so I would substitute tapioca or potato flour if you struggle with corn. It is very white in colour and quite chalky in texture.

5. *Lupin Flour:* Not widely used and it is listed as an allergen so I tend not to use it. However, it is a possibility for baking at home where you know no one has an allergy to it. It is a white powder and is best used in a combination with potato and tapioca flour.

6. *Potato Flour:* Works well with corn flour. It has a very fine, powder-like appearance and is bright white. This is a great one to have in the cupboard for cooking and thickening sauces and gravies.

7. *Quinoa Flour:* This flour is cream-coloured and is somewhat coarser than other flours. I use it in a combination with tapioca and corn flour. It has a nutty flavour so I quite like the note that it adds to savoury dishes.

8. *Rice Flour:* A heavy flour and quite coarse. It is possible to buy white and brown rice flour. It works well with, or as a substitute for, ground almonds. Again, this flour can taste quite gritty so it is best to use it in conjunction with others.

9. *Soya Flour:* Another flour that is used a lot in gluten-free baking, but in fact many people are allergic to it. I have excluded soya from this book for that very reason. For those of you who like to use it, again, it is white in appearance, has little taste of its own, but works well with a combination of corn and rice flour, or with teff and potato flour.

10. *Teff Flour:* A little-used flour, it tends to be more expensive than potato or corn flour but it is versatile. It is imported from Ethiopia, so is not locally grown. It works in a combination with other flours. Not very white in appearance and quite gritty. You can buy both brown and white teff flour. Either can be used in the recipes here.

11. *Tapioca Flour:* Another versatile flour and easy to find in health shops and some supermarkets. It is similar to corn flour in appearance and it marries well with flours like teff, corn or potato flour.

Gums: Gums are essential in gluten-free baking as they do the job of the gluten that is missing: they help to keep cakes and breads from falling apart. Xanthan gum and guar gum vary somewhat. Both come in the form of a fine powder. I use gum in my flour recipes but have also pointed out where extra gum needs to be added. Which gum is most appropriate depends on the other ingredients in the recipe. They can be sourced in most health food shops and some supermarkets.

How to cut chocolate: When you are cutting chocolate flapjacks or tray bakes that have hard chocolate on top, equip yourself with a jug of boiling water, a tea towel and a sharp knife. Dip your knife blade into the hot water and allow it a few moments to heat up. Wipe it swiftly on the tea towel to dry it and then cut your chocolate squares. The heat of the blade will melt through the chocolate, without snapping or breaking it.

Muffins: Muffins can be tricky. I admit to having made dreadful muffins in my time until I discovered the secret: never over mix a muffin. Always mix by hand, never with a mixer and stir very, very gently to combine the ingredients.

Pure oats: Always ensure that you use pure oats rather than 'regular' oats when baking for a coeliac. These have been processed in a very specific manner to avoid cross-contamination. However, be mindful that a very small minority of coeliacs cannot tolerate pure oats, so do check with your coeliac before presenting them with your oat cookies or granola.

Rolling out gluten-free pastry: Pastry is the bête noire of the gluten-free world, isn't it? We get so many phone calls in the bakery from wonderful home-bakers who cannot master pastry. I have a recipe here that is based on our pastry mix; all developed because of queries from you! I will stand up and say that my pastry mix will roll out beautifully for you and will not break or crack. However, I understand that some of you may be nervous around pastry and if so, a good trick is to put your ball of pastry between two pieces of cling film. Roll the pastry through the cling film. The pastry sticks to the underside of the cling film and doesn't fall apart, which is the classic gluten-free pastry issue. Then peel off the top layer of cling film gently and invert the piece of pastry over your pie dish and use the remaining piece of cling film to allow you to move the pastry and tuck it in. When it is in place as you need, then peel off the remaining piece of cling film and there you have it.

Separating eggs: For making meringues, you need egg whites without any yolks. If even the tiniest bit of egg yolk remains in your egg whites, then you need to start over as the yolk will prevent the whites from whipping up. You can now buy egg whites in a bottle, ready to go. The perfect solution! It also means you do not have to think creatively about how to use up your egg yolks afterwards.

Spoon measures: Buy yourself a little set of measuring spoons as they are so handy and you would be amazed at the difference in various tablespoons and how much they weigh. Make sure to use a level rather than a rounded measuring spoon for the recipes here.

Sponge cakes: Here's an old trick. If you're unsure if your sponge cake is baked, take it out of the oven and gently raise it to your ear. Be careful not to burn yourself! If you can hear a popping or gentle hissing sound then the sponge is not yet baked. If the sponge is silent, all is well and you can take it out of the oven and allow it to cool.

Sugar-free baking: These recipes are not based on a diabetic diet. However, we are mindful of the need for sugar-free recipes, so watch this space! Some of these recipes can be adapted for a sugar-free diet using apple puree, agave syrup or Xylitol, to name a few options. Feel free to experiment or drop us an email for advice.

Your oven: Begin a love affair with your oven and get to know its quirks and idiosyncrasies! Oven temperatures will always vary slightly from oven to oven. The oven temperatures I have included here are standard, but you may find that your oven is a little hotter or colder and you will need to tweak the temperature and baking time. It is just a case of watching and learning how your oven works. Fan ovens tend to have an overall even temperature, but non-fan ovens do not. Recipes are generally cooked at about 20°C less in a fan oven than a regular oven, but check the manual that came with it. The best approach for baking is to place a cake on the centre shelf. Also, always, always preheat your oven when baking. Cakes do not like to be in a cold oven.

Chapter 1

Regular Bakes and Basics

Denise's Delicious flour blend

This is a great, all-round white flour. If you are avoiding corn, then use tapioca flour instead. There are lots of decent white gluten-free/wheat-free flours on the market, but all perform differently. I have blended this to suit my recipes here.

....

Makes approximately 850g (2lb) flour blend

....

250g (10oz) rice flour

25g (1oz) tapioca flour

275g (11oz) potato flour

275g (11oz) corn flour

13g (½oz) teff flour

1 teaspoon gluten-free (GF) baking powder

1 teaspoon guar gum

Sieve all the ingredients into a bowl and mix well.

Savoury pastry

If you are nervous of handling gluten-free pastry (whether sweet or savoury) when starting off, using cling film is a great comfort (see p. 24). This pastry is great for quiches and savoury tarts.

Makes enough for 6 tartlets or for the base and top of a 13cm/5in pie

200g (8oz) Denise's Delicious flour blend (p. 28)

Pinch of salt

1 teaspoon xanthan gum

100g (4oz) butter/margarine, at room temperature

1 large egg

2 tablespoons cold water, if needed

Sieve the flour, salt and xanthan gum into a medium-sized bowl.

Cut the butter/margarine into cubes and add to the flour mixture. Using an electric mixer, on speed two, work the butter/margarine into the flour until it resembles breadcrumbs.

In a small bowl, beat the egg lightly with a fork.

Add the egg to the mixture and, using the mixer, bring together into a ball. One egg is sufficient for this and the mix should form into a ball. However, if the egg is not very large, then add the water one tablespoon at a time. Do not add the water if the mix does not need it, you do not want a sticky pastry.

Wrap in a piece of greaseproof paper and chill in the fridge for 30 minutes. When ready to roll out, roll onto a board floured with potato flour. If you are nervous about handling gluten-free pastry, then place it between two pieces of cling film and roll out.

Sweet pastry

If you are nervous working with pastry, you can use cling film (see p. 24). But don't worry, this recipe works so you will not need to resort to it!

Makes enough for 6 tartlets or for the base and top of a 13cm/5in pie

200g (8oz) Denise's Delicious flour blend (p. 28)

Pinch of salt

¾ teaspoon xanthan gum

100g (4oz) butter/margarine

50g (2oz) caster sugar

1 small egg

2 tablespoons water

Sieve the flour, salt and gum into a medium-sized bowl.

Cut the butter/margarine into cubes and add to the flour mixture. Using an electric mixer, on speed two, work the butter/margarine into the flour until it resembles breadcrumbs.

Mix the sugar into the flour mixture with a wooden spoon.

In a small bowl, beat the egg lightly with a fork.

Add the egg to the mixture and, using the mixer, beat well to bring together into a ball. One egg is sufficient for this and the mix should form into a ball. However, if the egg is not very large, then add the water one tablespoon at a time. Do not add the water if the mix does not need it, you do not want a sticky pastry.

Wrap in a piece of greaseproof paper and chill in the fridge for 30 minutes. When ready to roll out, roll onto a floured board. If you are nervous about handling gluten-free pastry, then place it between two pieces of cling film to roll out.

Filled flatbread

This flatbread is easy to make and the centre can be filled with a variety of ingredients, keeping everyone in the house happy.

Makes 4

Filling

1 large aubergine, thinly sliced

2 courgettes, thinly sliced

Salt and pepper

4 tablespoons olive oil, plus 2 for brushing

2 tablespoons oregano or rosemary, finely chopped

6 tablespoons sun-dried tomato paste

4 large tomatoes, thinly sliced

Bread

50g (2oz) quinoa flour

50g (2oz) corn flour

50g (2oz) buckwheat flour

75g (3oz) potato flour

75g (3oz) tapioca flour

1½ teaspoons salt

½ teaspoon GF baking powder

¾ teaspoon guar gum

1 large egg

3 tablespoons olive oil

180ml (6floz) water

Place the aubergine and courgettes in a bowl, season lightly, add four tablespoons of oil and toss. Arrange the vegetables on a large foil-lined baking tray. Sprinkle with the herbs and grill for 6–8 minutes until golden, then turn over and grill the other side until golden.

For the bread, put the flours, salt, baking powder and gum into a bowl and mix well.

Mix the egg, olive oil and water in a small bowl and whisk to combine.

Make a well in the centre of the flour and add the egg mixture in two batches, mixing with a round-bladed knife to a firm dough and adding a little more water if the mixture is too dry.

On a board, floured with potato flour, knead lightly until smooth.

Divide the dough into four pieces. Roll one piece out very thinly on a well-floured surface to an 18cm/7in round, turning the dough frequently so it does not stick to the surface. Shape the remaining pieces in the same way. If you are nervous about rolling the bread, place the piece of dough between two pieces of cling film and roll; when it is the right size, peel off the top piece of the cling film and lift the flatbread using the bottom piece of cling film.

Brush a large frying pan with a little olive oil and fry the flatbreads individually for about one minute on each side.

Brush each one with a little more oil and smear with some tomato paste, then arrange the aubergine, courgette and tomato slices on top. Season and fold over to serve.

Seeded brown soda bread

I have included a soda bread recipe rather than a yeast bread as baking a gluten-free yeast bread at home is dreadfully tricky and can go wrong very easily. Soda bread is much more manageable. The brownness of the rice flour, when used with the buckwheat and carob flours, gives the bread its brown colour.

50g (2oz) brown rice flour

100g (4oz) tapioca flour

100g (4oz) potato flour

100g (4oz) buckwheat flour

50g (2oz) carob flour

½ teaspoon xanthan gum

1 teaspoon GF baking powder

½ teaspoon cream of tartar

½ teaspoon bread soda

1 large egg

350ml (12floz) milk

2 tablespoons olive oil

1 tablespoon honey

1 tablespoon treacle

100g (4oz) mixed pumpkin seeds, sunflower seeds and poppy seeds

Preheat the oven to Gas Mark 6/200°C/400°F. Grease and line a 900g/2lb loaf tin with baking parchment, making sure to line the sides well.

Combine the rice, tapioca, potato, buckwheat and carob flours.

Add the gum, baking powder and cream of tartar and mix well. Sieve in the bread soda and mix again.

In a measuring jug, beat the egg and add the milk and oil. Whisk to combine. Add the honey and treacle and mix well. Pour the wet ingredients into the dry and mix with a metal spoon until fully combined. If the mixture seems very tight, add a little extra milk, one tablespoon at a time, and mix in. You aim is to have a texture like wet cement.

Spoon into the baking tin and smooth out.

With a sharp knife, gently cut an indentation down the centre of the loaf.

Sprinkle the seeds over the top of the bread and place in the centre of the preheated oven.

Bake for ten minutes at Gas Mark 6/200°C/400°F, then turn the oven down to Gas Mark 5/190°C/375°F. Bake for 30 minutes or until a skewer inserted comes out dry and the base of the bread sounds hollow when you remove it from the tin and tap it.

After removing the loaf from the tin, wrap it in a damp tea towel while it cools to keep the crust soft.

Quiche Lorraine

A French classic that is great fresh out of the oven, or the following day, cold or reheated.

1 quantity of savoury pastry (p. 29)

½ beaten egg for brushing pastry

6 rashers of smoked streaky bacon

300ml (10floz) double cream

1 large egg

3 large egg yolks

Black pepper

Preheat the oven to Gas Mark 6/200°C/400°F and grease a 23cm/9in round Pyrex pie dish.

Make the pastry according to the instructions on page 29.

Line the pie dish base and sides with the pastry and trim to fit exactly. Keep any extra pieces of pastry, as you may need them later.

Bake the pastry blind for 15 minutes in the centre of the oven. There is no need to use baking beans for gluten-free pastry (see p. 19).

Next, check for any holes that may have appeared in the pastry while it was baking or that you may have missed earlier. Fill any holes with a little of the spare pastry and then brush over with the beaten egg.

Turn the oven down to Gas Mark 4/180°C/350°F.

Snip the bacon into strips and cook it gently in a frying pan until the fat begins to run. The strips should remain pink and soft, not crispy.

Drain and leave to cool slightly on a piece of kitchen paper, before spreading over the bottom of the pastry case. Whisk together the cream, egg, yolks and pepper, then pour into the pastry case and place in the oven for 20 minutes. You will know when it is ready, as the filling will have set.

Remove from the oven and leave for 10 minutes before serving.

Savoury loaf

This savoury loaf is a recipe from a lovely lady in Brittany. It is a wonderful accompaniment to a glass of chilled white wine with friends.

125g (5oz) Denise's Delicious flour blend (p. 28)

1 teaspoon GF baking powder

½ teaspoon guar gum

60ml (2floz) vegetable oil

120ml (4floz) milk

4 large eggs

125g (5oz) olives, chopped and stoned

225g (9oz) ham, chopped

125g (5oz) Gruyère, grated

50g (2oz) chopped walnuts

Preheat the oven to Gas Mark 4/180°C/350°F. Line a 900g/2lb loaf tin with a baking liner or grease and cut baking parchment to fit.

Mix the flour, baking powder and gum until fully combined.

Separately, mix the oil, milk and eggs. Make a well in the centre of the dry ingredients, pour in the egg mixture and whisk well.

Next, add the olives, ham, cheese and walnuts and stir into the mixture. If the mixture seems very stiff, add a little extra milk and beat in.

Pour the mixture into the loaf tin and bake in the centre of the preheated oven for 45–50 minutes. Test with a skewer and it should come out dry.

When baked, gently turn out of the tin and cool on a wire rack.

To serve, slice thinly and cut each slice in half. Serve accompanied by a crisp white wine.

Pizza

We sell an enormous amount of our pizza bases directly from the bakery and they are great to have in the freezer for a quick supper solution. I know that working with yeast is time-consuming and tricky, but here is a good pizza recipe for those of you that want to give it a go. For everyone else, just give us a call!

Makes 4–5 x 150g bases or 6–7 x 100g bases

Base

580g (1lb 5oz) Denise's Delicious flour blend (p. 28)

½ teaspoon salt

40g (1½oz) margarine

15g (½oz) xanthan gum

25g (1oz) sugar

25g (1oz) dried yeast

420–480ml (14–16floz) warm water

1 tablespoon olive oil

Pizza sauce

2 x 400g (14oz) tins of tomatoes, drained

1 tablespoon lemon juice

1 tablespoon cider vinegar

1 teaspoon mixed herbs

1 teaspoon salt

¼ teaspoon ground black pepper

Toppings

Sliced pepperoni

Sliced mushroom

Grated mozzarella

Base

Sieve the flour and salt into a bowl.

Rub in the margarine.

Add the gum and sugar.

Separately, mix the yeast with 420ml (14floz) of the warm water.

Make a well in the centre of the dry ingredients and pour in the yeast and water mixture.

In an electric mixer, using a dough hook, beat until the dough forms a ball. If it is not forming a ball or is very dry or tough, gradually add the remaining warm water. You should end up with a soft, pliable dough that leaves the bowl clean.

Turn onto a board floured with a little potato flour, and knead this dough for around ten minutes, until smooth.

Oil the inside of the bowl with the olive oil and return the dough to the bowl and cover with a clean towel or cling film. Place the bowl somewhere warm and allow the dough to prove until it has doubled in size. If your kitchen is warm this should only take about 2 hours. The warmer your room, the quicker the dough will prove.

Remove the dough from the bowl once proved and divide into balls of 150g (5oz) for a 23cm/9in pizza or 100g (4oz) for an 18cm/7in pizza (see tips).

Knead lightly to make the underside of the pizza dough smooth. Then, with a rolling pin, roll the dough, turning it between each roll to prevent the pizza from sticking. Use plenty of potato flour on the board, dough and rolling pin to prevent sticking.

Place on a floured baking tray and prick the pizza base all over with a fork.

Preheat the oven to Gas Mark 6/200°C/400°F.

Pizza sauce
Place all the ingredients in a blender and zap until smooth. Spread generously on the pizza base, keeping in a little from the edges.

To finish
Cover with grated cheese, sliced pepperoni and mushrooms, or other toppings of your choice.

Cook in the hot oven and lift the pizza out with a fish slice to check that it is fully cooked underneath.

Tips

These pizza bases freeze really well and it can be very handy to have some already frozen so that you just need to top them as required.

For freezing, the bases should only be part baked. Follow all the steps listed above, but pop the bases into the oven without any toppings. Bake them until they are a very light golden colour and only partially cooked. This should take 4–5 minutes. The bases should hold their shape – you should be able to pick them up.

Allow the bases to cool on a wire rack and then they are ready to freeze. Store in the freezer, either in individual plastic bags or, if you are stacking the pizza bases, place a sheet of greaseproof paper between each base before putting them into a bag.

When topping, please make sure the pepperoni is gluten-free. Also, if using pre-grated cheese, check that it does not have wheat flour added.

Savoury drop scones with goats' cheese

Drop scones are a great substitute for bread or toast. They are wonderful as a savoury or sweet option. For sweet drop scones, substitute 25g (1oz) of caster sugar for the ¼ teaspoon of black pepper.

This should make 8–10 drop scones, depending on how generous you are with the mix for each scone!

75g (3oz) potato flour

65g (2½oz) corn flour

15g (½oz) teff flour

50g (2oz) tapioca flour

¾ teaspoon xanthan gum

1 teaspoon salt

1 teaspoon bread soda

2 teaspoons cream of tartar

¼ teaspoon freshly ground black pepper

1 large egg

170ml (6floz) milk

Butter/margarine for frying

To serve

25g (1oz) goats' cheese

Sieve the flours, gum, salt, bread soda and cream of tartar into a medium-sized bowl. Add the pepper and mix.

Whisk in the egg and milk until well combined.

Heat the butter/margarine in a heavy frying pan. Drop two tablespoons of the mixture onto the pan for each scone. Tiny bubbles will appear and when these burst, turn the scones over using a palette knife.

Cook the underside of each scone until golden brown, then remove and cool the scones on a wire rack.

Cut the goats' cheese into discs and place one on top of each scone.

Place on a baking tray under a preheated grill until the cheese is partially melted and lightly browned.

Serve with a side salad as a light lunch.

Fruit scones

There is nothing quite like fresh scones. Do them justice and eat them on the day of baking.

Makes 8–10 scones, depending on what size cutter you use

200g (8oz) Denise's Delicious flour blend (p. 28)

1 teaspoon GF baking powder

1 teaspoon xanthan gum

50g (2oz) margarine

50g (2oz) caster sugar

25g (1oz) dried Californian sultanas

2 large eggs

A little milk

Preheat the oven to Gas Mark 5/190°C/375°F.

Sieve the flour, baking powder and xanthan gum.

Rub in the margarine until the mixture resembles breadcrumbs.

Sieve the caster sugar and add to the dry ingredients.

Add the dried fruit.

Beat the eggs and add to the mixture. Bring together into a ball. If the mixture is a little stiff or does not form a ball, add a little milk to soften.

Turn onto a floured board and knead lightly until the underside of the dough is without cracks.

Press out with the palm of your hand and cut out scones using a round scone cutter – dip the cutter in potato flour before cutting each scone.

Place on a floured baking tray and brush the top of each scone with a little milk.

Bake in the centre of the oven for 15–20 minutes until brown. Turn the scones upside down for the final five minutes to finish cooking and ensure that they are baked to a golden colour underneath.

Cool on a wire rack and eat warm.

Buttermilk pancakes with blueberries & maple syrup

These are wonderful pancakes for weekend mornings. It is worth investing in a heavy griddle pan for the best result. The batter can be made the night before and stored in the fridge, then used the following morning.

Makes 3–4 pancakes

150g (6oz) Denise's Delicious flour blend (p. 28)

1 tablespoon GF baking powder

1 teaspoon salt

3 tablespoons caster sugar

2 large eggs

390ml (13floz) buttermilk

1 teaspoon vanilla extract

Butter/margarine to grease the pan

To serve

175g (7oz) blueberries

Maple syrup

Preheat the griddle pan (or heavy-based frying pan) for 1–2 minutes over a medium heat.

Sieve the flour, baking powder and salt into a medium-sized bowl and stir in the sugar.

In a separate bowl, beat the eggs with a whisk, then add the buttermilk and vanilla extract and whisk until fully combined.

Make a well in the centre of the dry ingredients and pour in the egg mixture. Using a whisk, beat well.

Melt the butter/margarine in the preheated pan and pour some batter into the centre of the pan. Tilt the pan to spread the batter until the pancake is approximately 10–12cm/4–4½in in diameter.

When the batter has set, flip the pancake using a palette knife or fish slice, and brown on the other side. Repeat until all the pancakes are cooked.

Serve warm with fresh blueberries and maple syrup.

Breton galettes with Raclette cheese & red peppers

A galette is a traditional Breton savoury crêpe made with buckwheat flour. If you feel like treating yourself, enjoy one of these with a glass of cider for lunch – it's a Breton tradition, no excuse needed! Raclette is a great cheese for melting. If you find it hard to come by, then Gruyère is a lovely substitute.

This should make 2–3 galettes, depending on how thin or thick you make them!

75g (3oz) buckwheat flour

25g (1oz) potato flour

¼ teaspoon guar gum

¼ teaspoon salt

1 large egg

1 tablespoon sunflower oil

240ml (8floz) milk (approx.)

50g (2oz) butter/margarine

4–6 thin slices Raclette cheese

Roasted red bell peppers as needed, chopped

Place the flours, gum and salt in a medium-sized bowl and mix well.

Break the egg in a measuring jug and beat with a fork. Add the oil and stir in.

Add the milk to the egg, approximately 240ml (8floz), until the total liquids measure 300ml (10floz). Whisk well to combine.

Pour a third of the liquid into the flour mixture and combine with a whisk. Continue until all the liquid has been added and the batter is fully blended without any lumps.

Place your frying pan over a medium heat and melt the butter/margarine. Pour about ½ cup of the batter into the centre of the pan. Lift the pan and then tilt and rotate it until the batter is evenly spread and forms a nice thin disc. Put it back on the heat. It should start bubbling after a few seconds. Turn the heat to low. Turn the galette over to brown lightly on both sides.

Place 1–2 slices of Raclette cheese on top of the galette and add some chopped pepper. Fold the crêpe and let the cheese melt and the pepper warm for 1–2 minutes.

Repeat until all the batter is used, stirring each time before pouring.

Cheese biscuits

A lovely biscuit for lunchboxes or with a cheese course at dinner. Keep in an airtight container or biscuit tin. Do check that your coeliac is happy to eat pure oats before serving.

Makes 12–16, depending on the thickness of the biscuits

50g (2oz) potato flour

25g (1oz) teff flour

25g (1oz) corn flour

100g (4oz) butter/margarine, at room temperature

½ teaspoon salt

½ teaspoon xanthan gum

200g (8oz) pure oats

75g (3oz) grated Parmigiano cheese

1 medium egg

3 tablespoons water

Preheat the oven to Gas Mark 3/165°C/325°F. Line a baking tray with baking parchment.

Sieve the flours into a medium-sized bowl.

Add the butter/margarine to the flours and rub together until the mixture resembles breadcrumbs.

Add the salt, gum, oats and cheese and mix with a metal spoon.

In a separate bowl, mix the egg with the water and whisk gently.

Add the egg and water to the dry ingredients and mix to a stiff dough.

Turn onto a board, floured with potato flour. Take half the dough and press gently with your hands to flatten.

With a floured rolling pin, roll out to an 18cm/7in circle. Using a square cookie cutter, cut out your biscuits – dip the cutter in potato flour before cutting each biscuit. If the biscuits are sticking to the board, slip a palette knife underneath to remove them gently from the board.

Repeat with the remaining dough until all the biscuits are cut. Gently place on a baking tray, leaving plenty of space in between.

Bake in the centre of the preheated oven until the biscuits are dry and golden in colour – approximately 15 minutes.

Cool on a wire rack and store in an airtight container.

Asparagus & Parmigiano savoury tart

Marcel Proust has a very famous description of asparagus in his In Search of Lost Time, *where he talks of its 'rainbow-loveliness' which is 'not of this world'! We hope that Proust approves of our use of asparagus in this recipe.*

1 quantity of savoury pastry (see p. 29)

½ beaten egg for brushing pastry

1 good-sized bundle of asparagus (8–9 spears)

300ml (10floz) cream

150ml (5floz) milk

4 large egg yolks

2 tablespoons freshly grated Parmigiano cheese

Salt and black pepper

Preheat the oven to Gas Mark 6/200°C/400°F and grease a 23cm/9in round Pyrex pie dish.

Make the pastry according to the instructions on page 29.

Line the pie dish base and sides with the pastry and trim to fit exactly. Keep any extra pieces of pastry as you may need them later.

Bake the pastry blind for 15 minutes in the centre of the oven. There is no need to use baking beans for gluten-free pastry (see p. 19).

Next, check for any holes that may have appeared in the pastry while it was baking or that you may have missed earlier. Fill any holes with a little of the spare pastry and then brush over with the beaten egg.

Turn the oven down to Gas Mark 4/180°C/350°F.

Steam the asparagus and leave to cool.

Whisk the cream, milk and egg yolks together, then add the grated Parmigiano and season.

Spoon the cooled asparagus into the pastry case, then pour the egg mixture over the asparagus. Bake in the oven for 25–30 minutes until puffed up and just set and browned.

Leave to cool for 10 minutes, then serve with a dressed green salad.

Granola

Granola is great for brunch and there is nothing as nice as a bowl of home-made granola in the centre of the table with some fresh fruit, natural yogurt and some local honey for a relaxed Sunday get together. Do check that your coeliac is happy to eat pure oats before serving.

500g (18oz) pure oats

25g (1oz) pumpkin seeds

25g (1oz) sunflower seeds

25g (1oz) linseed

75g (3oz) brown sugar

135ml (4½floz) sunflower oil

3 tablespoons honey

50g (2oz) dried dates, chopped and stoned

50g (2oz) dried figs, chopped

25g (1oz) flaked almonds

125g (5oz) sultanas

Preheat the oven to Gas Mark 3/165°C/325°F.

In a medium-sized bowl, mix the oats with the three seed types and the brown sugar.

In a small bowl, whisk the sunflower oil with the honey until blended.

Pour the oil and honey over the oats and seeds, stirring well to coat everything.

Spread on two baking trays or a large roasting dish and place in the centre of the preheated oven.

Bake for 30–40 minutes until golden brown. Stir every 10 minutes to ensure that the granola browns evenly.

Once baked, allow to cool.

Mix the dates, figs, flaked almonds and sultanas together.

Mix this into the cooled granola and pour into an airtight jar to store.

Chapter 2

Old Favourites with a Twist

Banana cake with passion fruit drizzle

Banana and passion fruit is a very pleasing combination. The passion fruit icing just finishes the cake beautifully and lends a touch of the exotic to our trusted banana bread. This recipe makes two one-pound loaves, so a handy size to slice for lunch boxes.

4 ripe bananas, mashed

225g (9oz) caster sugar

120ml (4floz) sunflower oil

2 large eggs

200g (8oz) Denise's Delicious flour blend (p. 28)

1½ teaspoons GF baking powder

1 teaspoon guar gum

Passion fruit icing

8 tablespoons icing sugar

2 tablespoons passion fruit pulp (from approx. 2 passion fruits)

Preheat the oven to Gas Mark 5/190°C/375°F. Grease two 1lb/450g loaf tins and line with baking parchment, or use loaf tin liners.

Mix the mashed bananas with the sugar and the sunflower oil.

Beat the eggs and add to the sugar, oil and mashed bananas.

In a separate bowl, sieve the flour, baking powder and guar gum and mix well. Add to the egg mixture and combine.

Pour the batter into the prepared tins.

Bake in the centre of the oven for 40–50 minutes, until they are golden brown and a skewer inserted comes out dry.

Turn out onto a wire tray and peel off the baking parchment.

For the passion fruit icing, sieve the icing sugar into a bowl and add the passion fruit pulp. If the mixture is too dry, add a teaspoon of water.

Blend into a paste and drizzle on the top of the cool banana cakes.

Old-style lemon & poppy seed Madeira cake

This is a traditional Madeira cake with a modern twist. Poppy seed is used very little in Irish baking but I feel it adds an interesting feature and marries well with the lemon.

100g (4oz) butter/margarine

100g (4oz) caster sugar

2 large eggs

50g (2oz) corn flour

50g (2oz) potato flour

50g (2oz) rice flour

½ teaspoon xanthan gum

1 teaspoon GF baking powder

Grated zest and juice of 1 lemon

15g (½oz) poppy seeds

To decorate

50g (2oz) icing sugar

Juice of 1 lemon

Preheat the oven to Gas Mark 5/190°C/375°F. Grease and line a 1lb/450g loaf tin with baking parchment.

Cream the butter/margarine and sugar until light and fluffy. Add the eggs one at a time and beat between each addition.

Sieve the flours, xanthan gum and baking powder together in a separate bowl, then add the flour mixture to the egg mixture in three batches, folding it in with a metal spoon rather than an electric mixer and mixing well between each addition. Finally, add the lemon juice, zest and the poppy seeds.

Scoop into the tin and bake in the centre of the oven for approximately 50 minutes or until a skewer comes out clean. Allow to cool in the tin before turning out.

While the cake is still hot, insert a skewer into several places on top of the cake. In a small bowl, sieve the icing sugar and stir in the lemon juice gradually, until blended. Pour this on top of the cake, allowing it to drizzle into the holes made by the skewer.

Marble cake

This cake is a trip down memory lane. Mum used to make this when I was little and I was fascinated at how she managed to make the cake all different colours. Of course I only wanted to eat the pink bits. I'm all grown up now so I'm happy to eat all the colours!

100g (4oz) butter/margarine

75g (3oz) caster sugar

2 large eggs

50g (2oz) corn flour

50g (2oz) potato flour

50g (2oz) rice flour

½ teaspoon xanthan gum

1 teaspoon GF baking powder

2 tablespoons milk (if needed)

1–2 drops natural green and red food colouring

1–2 drops vanilla extract

Preheat the oven to Gas Mark 5/190°C/375°F. Grease and line a 1lb/450g loaf tin with baking parchment.

Cream the butter/margarine and sugar until light and fluffy. Add the eggs one at a time and beat between each addition.

Sieve the flours, gum and baking powder together in a separate bowl, then add the flour to the egg mixture in three batches, folding it in with a metal spoon rather than an electric mixer, mixing well between each addition. The mixture should be a dropping consistency and if it seems tight, add some milk, half a tablespoon at a time, until the mixture softens.

Divide the creamed mixture into three small bowls. To the first bowl add 1–2 drops of red food colouring and stir well until the mixture becomes a soft pink colour. To the second bowl add 1–2 drops of green food colouring and mix well. To the last bowl add 1–2 drops of vanilla extract.

Fill the cake tin by alternating with a scoop of each different mixture until they have all been used up.

Bake in the centre of the oven for approximately 45 minutes or until a skewer comes out clean. Leave to cool in the tin before turning out. When the cake is cold and you cut it, you will have a marbled effect of the pink, green and cream colours.

Softly spiced gingerbread

Thanks to Connie, our bakery manager, for sharing her mum's original gingerbread recipe with me. Here's my gluten-free version of it.

300g (12oz) Denise's Delicious flour blend (p. 28)

½ teaspoon salt

1 teaspoon GF baking powder

1 teaspoon ground cinnamon

1 teaspoon bread soda

1 teaspoon ground ginger

100g (4oz) sugar

2 large eggs

6 tablespoons treacle

100g (4oz) melted butter/margarine

250ml (8½floz) buttermilk or sour milk

To decorate

100g (4oz) icing sugar

60–90ml (2–3floz) water

Preheat the oven to Gas Mark 5/190°C/375°F. Grease a 2lb/900g loaf tin and line with a baking liner or else line the tin with baking parchment.

Sieve the flour, salt, baking powder, cinnamon and bread soda into a medium-sized bowl. Then add the ginger and the sugar. Mix well with a wooden spoon and set aside.

In a large bowl, beat the eggs and add the treacle, melted butter/margarine and buttermilk. Beat well with a whisk.

Add the flour ingredients to the wet ingredients in four batches, beating well between each addition. The mix should be smooth, without any lumps. If there are lumps, set aside for 1 minute and then whisk vigorously.

Fill the baking tin and bake in the preheated oven on the centre shelf for approximately 40 minutes or until an inserted skewer comes out dry.

Allow the cake to cool for 5–10 minutes in the cake tin, then remove to a wire rack.

To decorate

When the cake is completely cold, prepare the icing by putting the sieved icing sugar into a small bowl. Add the water a tablespoon at a time and mix with a spoon until fully blended to a honey-like consistency. Make sure there are no lumps. Pour over the cake.

Traditional cherry & almond cake

This is another cake that my mum used to make for me when I was little and I absolutely adore it – I really do not make it enough! To ensure that your cherries do not sink, follow Mum's steps below and make sure to wash the syrup off the cherries, as it is the syrup that causes them to sink to the bottom of the cake.

100g (4oz) butter/margarine

100g (4oz) caster sugar

2 large eggs

50g (2oz) potato flour

50g (2oz) corn flour

50g (2oz) rice flour

1 teaspoon xanthan gum

1 teaspoon GF baking powder

2 teaspoons almond essence

100g (4oz) natural red glacé cherries

50g (2oz) ground almonds

Preheat the oven to Gas Mark 5/190°C/375°F. Grease and line a 1lb/450g loaf tin with baking parchment.

Cream the butter/margarine and sugar until light and fluffy.

Beat the eggs one at a time into the creamed mixture.

Sieve the flours, gum and baking powder together in a separate bowl and mix well.

Fold the flour mixture into the egg mixture two tablespoons at a time, then mix in the almond essence.

Wash the cherries in hot water. Dry them and chop roughly.

Roll the cherries in the ground almonds to coat them.

Add the cherries and ground almonds to the cake mix and fold them in.

Bake in the loaf tin for 30–40 minutes or until a skewer inserted into the centre of the cake comes out dry.

Remove from the oven when baked and leave for 5 minutes in the tin before turning out onto a wire rack to cool.

Easter Simnel cake

This is a very traditional take on an Easter cake. I like to liven it up with some fluffy yellow chicks on top of the cake or some speckled chocolate eggs.

150g (6oz) butter/margarine

150g (6oz) brown sugar

3 large eggs, beaten

200g (8oz) Denise's Delicious flour blend (p. 28)

½ teaspoon GF baking powder

½ teaspoon ground mixed spice

Finely grated zest of 1 lemon

75g (3oz) raisins

75g (3oz) sultanas

40g (1½oz) mixed peel, chopped

450g/1lb marzipan (p. 198)

3 tablespoons apricot jam

Preheat the oven to Gas Mark 2/150°C/300°F. Grease and line a deep 20cm/8in diameter round cake tin with baking parchment.

Place the butter/margarine and sugar in a bowl and cream together with an electric mixer until pale, light and fluffy. Gradually beat in the eggs.

Sieve together the flour, baking powder and mixed spice and fold into the creamed mixture.

Stir in the lemon zest, raisins, sultanas and mixed peel, mixing evenly.

Spoon half the mixture into the prepared tin and smooth out to level it.

Roll out 250g (9oz) of the marzipan to a 20cm/8in round and place over the mixture in the tin. Add the remaining cake mixture and smooth the top. Bake the cake for 2¼–2¾ hours, or until firm and golden. Leave to cool in the tin for 30 minutes, then turn out onto a wire rack to finish cooling.

Brush the top of the cake with apricot jam. Roll out two-thirds of the remaining marzipan to a round to cover the top of the cake. Use a knife to mark a lattice design in the surface and pinch the edges to decorate.

Roll the remaining marzipan into eleven small balls and decorate the edge of the cake. Place under a hot grill for 30–40 seconds to brown lightly. Cool before serving.

Black Forest gateau

Black Forest gateau is a classic cake and there are many versions that don't do it credit. I hope you agree with me that this recipe does!

Sponge

5 large eggs

150g (6oz) caster sugar

25g (1oz) corn flour

25g (1oz) potato flour

½ teaspoon guar gum

½ teaspoon GF baking powder

50g (2oz) cocoa powder, sieved

75g (3oz) butter/ margarine, melted

Filling

5–6 tablespoons Kirsch

510ml (17floz) double cream

450g (1lb) tinned black cherries, chopped

To decorate

200g (8oz) dark chocolate

15–20 fresh cherries, preferably with stems

Preheat the oven to Gas Mark 5/190°C/375°F. Grease three deep 18cm/7in diameter round cake tins and line the bases with baking parchment.

Place the eggs and sugar in a large mixing bowl and beat with an electric mixer for about 10 minutes until the mixture is thick and pale.

Separately, sieve together the flours, gum, baking powder and cocoa powder three times to ensure there are no lumps, then sieve again into the whisked mixture. Fold in very gently, then slowly trickle in the melted butter/ margarine and continue to fold in gently.

Divide the mixture between the tins and smooth the surfaces with a pallet knife. Bake in the centre of the oven for about 25 minutes, or until springy to the touch.

Leave in the tins for about 5 minutes, then turn onto a wire rack, gently peel off the lining paper and leave to cool.

Lay the sponges on an even work surface. Sprinkle the three layers with the Kirsch to moisten the sponge.

In a large bowl, whip the cream until it forms soft peaks. Transfer two-thirds of the cream to another bowl and stir in the chopped cherries. Place a layer of cake on a serving plate and spread over half of the cherry cream. Top with another layer of cake and the rest of the cherry cream, finishing with a layer of cake.

Use the remaining whipped cream to cover the top of the gateau, spreading it evenly with a knife.

To decorate the gateau with chocolate shavings, melt the chocolate in a bowl over a pan of hot water, then spread the chocolate out on a plastic chopping board and allow it to set.

Using a long sharp knife, scrape along the surface of the chocolate to make thin shavings and use these to decorate the top.

Finally, arrange the cherries on top of the gateau.

Mocha Battenberg cake

Battenbergs are always impressive because, when cut, the alternating colours look great. This is not very difficult to make but everyone will think you are exceptionally accomplished!

25g (1oz) tapioca flour

50g (2oz) corn flour

25g (1oz) potato flour

1 teaspoon GF baking powder

1 teaspoon guar gum

100g (4oz) butter/margarine, softened

100g (4oz) caster sugar

2 large eggs

50g (2oz) ground hazelnuts

2 teaspoons coffee essence

1 tablespoon cocoa powder

To finish

7 tablespoons apricot jam, warmed and sieved

200g (8oz) marzipan (see p. 198)

50g (2oz) ground hazelnuts

Sieved icing sugar, to roll out marzipan

Ground hazelnuts, to decorate

Preheat the oven to Gas Mark 5/190°C/375°F. Grease an 18cm/7in square cake tin, making sure to grease the corners well, and line the base with baking parchment. Prepare a thick piece of tinfoil to fit the width and height of the cake tin. Position the strip of foil down the centre so that two different mixtures can be cooked separately in the tin.

Sieve the flours, baking powder and gum together and mix well. Place the butter/margarine and sugar in a separate bowl and beat until fluffy. Gradually beat in the eggs, then fold in the flour. Transfer half the mixture to another bowl.

Stir the ground hazelnuts into one half of the cake mixture and the coffee essence into the other half. Then sieve the cocoa powder into the hazelnut mixture and mix well.

Place the coffee-flavoured cake mixture into one half of the tin, then spoon the hazelnut-flavoured cake mixture into the other half, keeping the two mixes separate. Smooth the surfaces of both mixtures with a palette knife.

Bake for 30–35 minutes or until a skewer inserted into the centre of both halves comes out clean. Leave the cakes to cool in the tin for about 5 minutes, then turn out onto a wire rack, peel off the lining paper, separate the cakes and leave to cool completely.

When cold, start assembling the Battenberg. Cut each cake in half lengthways (so that you have two coffee layers and two chocolate layers). Take one portion of the coffee-flavoured cake and brush along one long side with a little apricot jam. Sandwich this surface with a portion of the chocolate-hazelnut-flavoured cake. Brush the top of the cake with apricot jam and position the other portion of the coffee-flavoured cake on top of the hazelnut base. Again, brush this layer with apricot jam and sandwich the final layer of hazelnut-flavoured cake on top. Set aside.

Knead the marzipan on the work surface to soften, then knead in the ground hazelnuts until evenly blended.

On the work surface, lightly dusted with icing sugar, roll out the marzipan into a rectangle large enough to wrap around the cake, excluding the ends.

Brush the cake with apricot jam, then lay the marzipan on top of the cake. Wrap the marzipan around the cake, sealing the edge neatly. Place the cake on a serving plate, seal-side down, and pinch the edges of the marzipan to give an attractive finish. Score the top surface with a knife and sprinkle with ground hazelnuts.

Mother's Day strawberry & mascarpone cream Victoria sponge

I always feel spring is coming when Mother's Day has arrived. Even if the weather doesn't oblige, I like to bake a cake that invokes springtime. This is a lovely cake for a family Sunday lunch. If you do not like to use mascarpone cheese, then use all freshly whipped cream.

150g (6oz) butter/margarine, at room temperature

125g (5oz) caster sugar

3 large eggs

50g (2oz) potato flour

50g (2oz) corn flour

50g (2oz) tapioca flour

1 teaspoon GF baking powder

½ teaspoon guar gum

To decorate

150ml (5floz) whipping cream

225g (9oz) mascarpone cheese

3 tablespoons icing sugar

1 punnet of strawberries, washed, hulled and chopped

Extra icing sugar for dusting

Preheat the oven to Gas Mark 5/190°C/375°F.

Grease two 20cm/8in sandwich tins and line the bases with baking parchment.

With an electric mixer, cream the butter/margarine with the sugar until light and fluffy.

In a separate bowl, beat the eggs lightly.

Add the eggs, a little at a time, to the butter/margarine mixture. Beat between each addition.

Into another bowl, sieve the flours, baking powder and gum, and mix until blended.

Using a spoon rather than a mixer, fold the flour into the egg mixture in three or four batches. Make sure one batch is folded in before adding the next one.

If the mixture seems a little tight – i.e. too stiff and does not drop easily off a spoon – then add 1–2 teaspoons of warm water. Add one at a time and mix it in. This will loosen the mixture.

Divide evenly between the two tins and smooth the surface with the back of a palette knife.

Bake in the preheated oven on the centre shelf for 25 minutes or so – when ready the sponges should be golden brown and springy.

Remove from the oven and leave to sit in the tins for 1–2 minutes before turning out onto a wire cooling tray. It is easier to do this if you first loosen around the edges with a flat knife.

Peel off the baking parchment and allow to cool.

To decorate

When the sponge is cool, whip the cream lightly. In a separate bowl, beat the mascarpone cheese and sieve in the icing sugar, beating until fully blended.

Add the whipped cream and mix in.

Place one sponge with its bottom facing upwards on a serving plate. Spread the mascarpone filling generously onto this and sprinkle with halved strawberries. Hold some strawberries back for the top of the cake.

Sandwich the second sponge snugly on top of the first.

Dust the top with icing sugar and arrange a pile of strawberry segments in the centre.

Peach crumble

This is a really lovely variation on traditional apple crumble. Using peaches adds a summery note to a crumble that is traditionally autumnal. Chestnut flour marries well with this recipe adding a subtle hint of chestnut to bring out the flavour of the peaches.

580g (1lb 5oz) fresh peaches

100g (4oz) brown sugar

1 teaspoon allspice

60ml (2floz) water

Grated zest of 1 lemon

Margarine for greasing

50g (2oz) potato flour

50g (2oz) corn flour

50g (2oz) chestnut flour

75g (3oz) butter/margarine

75g (3oz) caster sugar

Preheat the oven to Gas Mark 5/190°C/375°F and bring a pot of water to the boil.

Gently score the peaches and then submerge them in the pot of boiled water. This will cause the skin to wrinkle. Allow them to sit in the water for approximately 1 minute, then remove and peel with a sharp knife. The peaches will be hot, so be careful!

Stone and slice the peaches. Simmer them with the brown sugar, allspice, water and lemon zest in a covered pan until soft.

Fill a greased 1 litre pie dish with the fruit.

Sieve the flours together and then rub the butter/ margarine into the flour until it resembles fine breadcrumbs.

Add the caster sugar and stir well, then sprinkle the mixture over the peaches in the pie dish.

Bake in the oven for 30–40 minutes until the crumble is golden brown.

When baked, serve warm with a scoop of vanilla ice cream.

Pear & ginger tarte tatin

Apple tarte tatin is a traditional French recipe that works really nicely with pears. Gluten-free pastry has traditionally been horrendously difficult but I promise that this recipe will work for you!

1 quantity of sweet pastry (see p. 30)

12 ripe pears (approx.)

125g (5oz) butter/margarine

200g (8oz) caster sugar

¾ teaspoon ground ginger

Whipped cream to serve

Heat the oven to Gas Mark 6/200°C/400°F. Grease a 20cm/8in pie plate very well, making sure all the sides are well covered.

Make the pastry according to the instructions on page 30.

While the pastry is chilling, peel, core and halve the pears.

Slice the butter/margarine and line the bottom of a cast-iron pan (with an ovenproof handle) with it and put over a gentle heat.

Sprinkle the sugar and ginger on top.

Pack the pears snugly on the pan, as they shrink when cooked. Lie them with the cut side facing up as this makes the tart look better when it is turned out.

As the butter/margarine melts, it will caramelise with the sugar. It will begin to bubble between the pears and turn honey-coloured in approximately 15–20 minutes. Keep the heat low as it can burn easily.

Shift the pan to the side of the ring if the pears are cooking too much in the centre.

Take off the heat, but remember, as this is a cast-iron pan, it will continue to cook. If it has become too hot and is close to boiling, lower the base of the pan into cool water.

As the mixture cools, the caramel will set and the pears will shrink.

Roll out the pastry on a board floured with a little potato flour, leaving the pastry slightly larger than the pan, and put it on top of the pears, tucking the extra pastry in around the edge of the pan.

Place into the oven and then bake for approximately 20 minutes, until the pastry is golden brown.

Remove from the oven and allow to cool fully before turning out.

Turning this out can be tricky so it is best to heat the bottom of the pan very slightly to loosen the caramel, before turning it. This will help to hold the shape of the pie.

Place a serving plate on top of the pan and then invert it, placing the plate on a countertop with the pan on top. The tart should fall out onto the plate. The pastry will be on the base of the plate and the caramelised pears on top.

Serve with whipped cream.

Caribbean fruit flan

A flan is a wonderful lost treasure! I really don't know why flans have fallen out of fashion. Hopefully, you have a flan tin at the bottom of your cake tin pile. If not, you must procure one and guard it!

75g (3oz) Denise's Delicious flour blend (p. 28)

1 teaspoon GF baking powder

3 large eggs, at room temperature

65g (2½oz) caster sugar

1 teaspoon vanilla extract

For the filling and topping

300ml (10floz) whipping cream

1 fresh pineapple, chopped (cut it on a plate to be sure to catch the juice)

Fresh mango and kiwi, chopped

Preheat the oven to Gas Mark 5/190°C/375°F. Grease an 18cm/7in flan tin thoroughly.

Sieve the flour and baking powder and mix well.

In a separate bowl, whisk the eggs lightly with an electric mixer. Add the sugar and vanilla extract and whip on a high speed.

Add several tablespoons of the flour to the mix and fold in by hand with a metal spoon. Repeat until all the flour has been added.

Pour into the flan tin and bake in the centre of the oven until golden brown and springy. This should take 15–20 minutes.

Once removed from the oven, turn onto a wire cooling tray and gently tap the bottom of the tin to release the cake.

If it doesn't release easily, then turn the flan over and gently run a knife (not a serrated knife, ideally a palette knife) around the edges to release the flan. Then shake the sponge out gently.

Leave to cool fully.

Just before serving, whip the cream gently until soft peaks form. Add two teaspoons of pineapple juice and mix in.

Place the sponge on a serving plate and drizzle with some pineapple juice. This is to moisten the flan, you do not want it to be sodden, so do not overdo it. Spoon whipped cream onto the flan base and pile the chopped fruit on top.

Swiss roll with zesty grapefruit curd

Do not be put off by the grapefruit filling – it offers a really good contrast to the sweetness of the sponge. However, if it is too much for you, you can substitute orange, which is a gentler flavour.

100g (4oz) Denise's Delicious flour blend (p. 28)

1 teaspoon GF baking powder

¼ teaspoon guar gum

4 large eggs, at room temperature

100g (4oz) caster sugar

Grapefruit curd

Juice of 1 small pink grapefruit

3 large eggs

50g (2oz) sugar

1 tablespoon pink grapefruit zest, finely grated

Pinch of salt

4 tablespoons butter/ margarine, cut into small pieces and softened

Preheat the oven to Gas Mark 5/190°C/375°F. Grease and line a 25cm x 30cm/10in x 12in Swiss roll tin with baking parchment.

Sieve the flour, baking powder and gum and mix well.

Separate the eggs and whisk the whites until stiff, then add 25g (1oz) of sugar.

In a separate bowl, whisk the egg yolks and remaining 75g (3oz) of sugar until pale and creamy. When you lift the beaters out of the mixture, they should hold a trail in the mixture for 3–4 seconds.

Now carefully fold the egg yolk mixture into the egg white mixture. Use a metal spoon and do this by hand, not by machine.

Add several tablespoons of flour to the mix and fold in gently by hand with a metal spoon. Repeat until all the flour is added and ensure that no flour is lodged at the bottom of the bowl.

Pour into the Swiss roll tin. Once it is all in, tilt the tin back and forth until the mixture has filled the four corners.

Gently place in the centre of the oven and allow to bake for 12–15 minutes until golden brown and springy.

While the sponge is cooking, prepare everything for the rolling operation. Spread a damp tea towel on a flat surface (and have a second one ready for later). On top of the tea towel place a sheet of baking parchment that is slightly larger than the baking tin.

As soon as the Swiss roll is baked, remove from the oven and, holding the sides of the lining, turn it out onto the prepared baking parchment.

Now carefully and gently strip off the lining parchment.

Cover with a clean, damp towel and leave for a couple of minutes, then remove the damp towel. Then, with one of the shorter edges of the cake nearest to you, make a small incision about 2½cm (1in) from the edge, cutting right across the cake but not too deeply; this will help you when you start to roll.

Start by rolling this 2½cm/1in piece over and away from you and continue to roll, using the paper to help you roll the whole cake up by pulling it up behind it as it rolls. When it is completely rolled up, hold the paper around the cake for a few seconds, then transfer the rolled cake to a wire cooling tray.

Make the grapefruit curd (see below) and allow to cool.

When the Swiss roll is cool, gently unroll it. Do not force the unrolling – it will not be completely flat.

With a palette knife, gently spread the grapefruit curd filling inside the Swiss roll and then roll the Swiss roll back into its rolled position.

Trim 2cm off the edge of the Swiss roll with a sharp serrated knife, to tidy the edges.

Dust with icing sugar and serve.

Grapefruit curd

Bring the grapefruit juice to a boil in a small saucepan over a medium heat. Reduce the heat and simmer until the juice is reduced by half. Allow to cool.

Whisk together the eggs, sugar, reduced grapefruit juice, grapefruit zest and salt in a bowl over a pot of water on a medium heat, whisking constantly, until thickened. This will take 6–7 minutes. If your curd is not thickening (due to too much fruit juice), then add another egg yolk and beat in well whilst over the heat.

Remove from the heat and whisk in the butter/margarine until melted.

Pour the mixture through a fine sieve into a bowl. This will remove any fleshy parts of the grapefruit.

Cover the surface of the curd with a piece of greaseproof paper, and refrigerate until cool.

Chapter 3

Contemporary Cakes

Buttermilk cake with strawberry buttercream

My sister Louise made this cake recently for our Father's Day get together. We were all enthralled at how wonderful it tasted. I think the buttermilk is the secret ingredient. I hope you enjoy my version of Louise's scrumptious recipe.

For the cake

200g (8oz) butter/margarine

315g (12½oz) caster sugar

100g (4oz) corn flour

100g (4oz) rice flour

100g (4oz) potato flour

1 teaspoon GF baking powder

½ teaspoon salt

½ teaspoon bread soda

¾ teaspoon xanthan gum

4 large eggs

300ml (10floz) buttermilk

2 tablespoons lemon juice

1 tablespoon lemon zest

1 teaspoon vanilla extract

For the icing

200g (8oz) butter/margarine, at room temperature

1 teaspoon vanilla extract

50g (2oz) fresh strawberries

450g (1lb) icing sugar

60ml (2floz) whipping cream

To decorate

Fresh strawberries

Preheat the oven to Gas Mark 5/190°C/375°F. Flour and grease two 20cm/8in round cake tins.

In a medium-sized bowl, using an electric mixer, cream the butter/margarine and sugar together until light and fluffy. Sieve the flours, baking powder, salt, bread soda and gum into a bowl. Then mix the flours into the butter/margarine.

In a separate bowl, whisk the eggs together with the buttermilk, lemon juice, lemon zest and vanilla extract.

Slowly mix the wet ingredients into the dry by hand, or with the mixer on speed one, until the batter is combined.

Divide the batter equally between the two cake tins.

Bake for about 30 minutes or until a skewer inserted comes out clean.

Allow the cakes to cool for 5–10 minutes in the baking tins, then carefully turn them out onto a wire rack. Allow to cool completely before decorating.

To decorate

Using an electric mixer, cream the butter/margarine, vanilla extract, fresh strawberries (they mash as you mix) and icing sugar in a medium-sized bowl. Once smooth, turn the mixer to a medium speed and slowly mix in the whipping cream until light and fluffy.

When the cakes are cold, sandwich them together with one third of the strawberry icing. Then use the remainder to decorate the top and sides of the cake.

Top off with halved strawberries, leaving the green leaves on the fruit for colour.

Red velvet cake

This dramatic cake also makes a wonderful dessert for a glamorous dinner party!

For the cake

165g (6½oz) butter/
margarine at room
temperature, chopped

340g (13½oz) caster
sugar

3 large eggs

275g (11oz) Denise's
Delicious flour blend
(p. 28)

1 teaspoon guar gum

½ teaspoon GF baking
powder

½ teaspoon bread soda

75g (3oz) cocoa powder

120ml (4floz) warm water

120ml (4floz) milk

3 teaspoons instant
coffee powder

½ teaspoon natural red
food colouring

To decorate

50g (2oz) dark eating
chocolate, chopped

50g (2oz) butter/
margarine, chopped

25g (1oz) icing sugar

300ml (10floz) cream,
whipped, for the filling

Preheat the oven to Gas Mark 5/190°C/375°F. Grease two deep 20cm/8in round cake tins and line the bases with baking parchment.

Beat the butter/margarine and sugar in a medium-sized bowl with an electric mixer until light and fluffy and add the eggs one at a time, beating well after each addition.

Sieve the flour, gum, baking powder and bread soda. Make sure that there are no lumps in the bread soda.

Next add the cocoa to the flour mix and sieve this mixture three times to ensure there are no lumps.

Mix the water and milk with the coffee powder and stir to dissolve.

Fold the flour and cocoa powder into the butter/margarine mixture in three or four batches, mixing well between each addition.

Add the coffee mixture and mix again.

Finally, add the red food colouring and ensure it is blended in completely.

Pour into the baking tins and bake in the oven for about 45 minutes. Check that the centre of the cake is firm and that an inserted skewer comes out dry. Turn the cakes onto a wire rack to cool, taking them out of the baking tins and removing the parchment.

To decorate

For the rich chocolate icing, combine the chocolate and butter/margarine in a heatproof bowl over a saucepan of simmering water on a moderate heat. Sieve the icing sugar and add in, stirring until smooth. Remove from the heat once fully melted and combined. Cool at room temperature until spreadable, stirring occasionally while cooling.

If the frosting is not thickening enough, sieve in some additional icing sugar and stir in.

Sandwich the cold cakes with whipped cream and top with the rich chocolate icing.

American-style frosted chocolate cake

This is a simple chocolate cake that whips up easily and feels very American! It works well as cupcakes too (makes approximately 15) and the icing can be piped on to finish.

For the cake

25g (1oz) cocoa powder

1 teaspoon bread soda

510ml (17floz) water

600g (1lb 7oz) caster sugar

225g (9oz) butter/margarine at room temperature, chopped

450g (1lb) Denise's Delicious flour blend (p. 28)

1 teaspoon GF baking powder

1 teaspoon xanthan gum

4 large eggs, beaten lightly

Fudge frosting

75g (3oz) butter/margarine

90ml (3floz) water

100g (4oz) caster sugar

200g (8oz) icing sugar

25g (1oz) cocoa powder

To decorate

White chocolate curls

Preheat the oven to Gas Mark 5/190°C/375°F. Grease a round 27cm/10½in diameter baking tin and line the base with baking parchment.

Sieve the cocoa powder and bread soda together and put aside.

Combine the water, sugar and butter/margarine in a medium-sized saucepan, then stir over a low heat, without boiling, until the sugar dissolves. Stir in the cocoa and bread soda.

Bring to the boil, then reduce the heat and allow to simmer, uncovered, for 5 minutes.

Transfer the mixture to a large bowl and allow to cool to room temperature.

Sieve the flour, baking powder and gum into a separate bowl.

Whisk the eggs and add the flour mixture gradually, whisking between additions. Add this to the cocoa mixture and whisk until smooth.

Pour into the baking tin and bake in the oven for about 50 minutes. Gently insert a skewer into the centre of the cake to check it is fully baked. If baking as cupcakes they will require just 15–20 minutes to bake.

Allow the cake to stand in the tin for 10 minutes before turning out onto a wire rack. Turn the cake top side up to cool.

To decorate

To make the frosting, combine the butter/margarine, water and caster sugar in a small saucepan and stir over a low heat, without boiling, until the butter/margarine melts.

Sieve the icing sugar and cocoa powder into a medium-sized bowl, then gradually stir in the hot butter/margarine mixture.

Cover and refrigerate for about 20 minutes until the frosting thickens.

Remove the frosting from the fridge and whip with a wooden spoon until spreadable.

Using a palette knife, spread it over the cake and sprinkle with white chocolate curls.

Angel food cake

I am a big believer in the power of angels so it's fitting to include this recipe.

For the cake

25g (1oz) rice flour

50g (2oz) potato flour

50g (2oz) corn flour

½ teaspoon xanthan gum

1 teaspoon GF baking powder

1 teaspoon cream of tartar

200g (8oz) caster sugar

10 large egg whites

1 teaspoon vanilla extract

For the frosting

100g (4oz) caster sugar

60ml (2floz) water

2 large egg whites

2 teaspoons golden syrup

½ teaspoon vanilla extract

To decorate

15g (½oz) desiccated coconut

15g (½oz) chopped pistachio nuts

Preheat the oven to Gas Mark 5/190°C/375°F. Grease a 25cm/10in round cake tin and line the base with baking parchment.

Sieve the flours, gum, baking powder and cream of tartar. Add 50g (2oz) of the sugar and mix well to get rid of any lumps.

Whisk the egg whites until stiff and gradually whisk in the remaining sugar, a tablespoon at a time, until the mixture is thick and glossy.

Fold the flour mixture into the egg whites, one spoon at a time until combined. Add the vanilla extract and stir gently to combine.

Spoon the mixture into the tin and smooth out the top with a pallet knife.

Bake for 35–40 minutes in the centre of the oven until risen and golden. Check by inserting a skewer – it should come out dry.

Remove from the oven, invert the cake onto a wire rack and leave to cool.

To finish

To make the frosting, heat the sugar and water in a small pan until the sugar dissolves. Increase the heat and boil until the temperature reaches 115°C/240°F on a sugar thermometer. As soon as the mixture reaches this temperature, remove from the heat.

Whisk the egg whites until stiff. Pour the sugar syrup in a steady stream into the centre of the egg whites, whisking continuously, until thick and glossy. Beat in the golden syrup and vanilla extract and continue beating for 5 minutes until the frosting is cooled.

Place the cake on a turntable and coat with the frosting, using a palette knife to make a swirling pattern and peak effect.

To decorate, sprinkle the coconut and pistachios over the top of the cake.

Store in the fridge until ready to serve.

Coffee & butterscotch gateau

I decided to keep the butterscotch icing on the side here, as it is quite sweet and not necessarily to everyone's taste.

For the cake

200g (8oz) butter/margarine at room temperature, chopped

200g (8oz) demerara sugar

2 large eggs, lightly beaten

165g (6½oz) Denise's Delicious flour blend (p. 28)

1 teaspoon GF baking powder

½ teaspoon guar gum

1 tablespoon golden syrup

1 teaspoon instant coffee powder

1 tablespoon hot water

120ml (4floz) milk

Butterscotch icing

50g (2oz) butter/margarine

100g (4oz) firmly packed dark brown sugar

60ml (2floz) milk

200g (8oz) icing sugar, sieved

To decorate

300ml (10floz) whipping cream

Preheat the oven to Gas Mark 5/190°C/375°F. Grease a deep 20cm/8in round cake tin with a removable base. Line the base with baking parchment.

In a medium-sized bowl, cream the butter/margarine and sugar with an electric mixer.

Add the eggs gradually, beating between additions with the mixer on a medium speed.

Sieve the flour, baking powder and gum and add to the butter mixture in three batches, beating between each addition.

Beat in the golden syrup.

Mix the coffee powder with the hot water. Add the milk and mix to fully dissolve the coffee powder.

Add this coffee mixture to the cake mixture and beat with a metal spoon to combine fully.

Pour the mixture into the prepared tin.

Bake in the centre of the oven for about 1 hour, checking by inserting a skewer into the centre. When it is fully baked the skewer should be dry when removed. Allow the cake to sit in the tin for 10 minutes and then turn out by releasing the bottom and place onto a wire rack to cool. Cakes are at their most delicate at this stage, so do be careful.

To finish

To make the butterscotch icing, heat the butter/margarine, brown sugar and milk in a small saucepan, stirring constantly, without boiling, until the sugar dissolves, then remove immediately from the heat. Add the icing sugar and stir until smooth.

When the cake is cold split it into three layers, using a large serrated knife. Place one layer on a serving plate and spread with a third of the cream. Repeat with the second layer. Cover the top cake layer with the remaining cream.

Serve with the butterscotch icing in a jug to pour over the sliced cake.

St Valentine's Day
white chocolate sponge

You have to make this in a heart-shaped tin, even if you are baking it for yourself!

For the cake

150g (6oz) butter/
margarine, at room
temperature

125g (5oz) caster sugar

3 large eggs

50g (2oz) potato flour

50g (2oz) corn flour

50g (2oz) tapioca flour

1 teaspoon GF baking
powder

½ teaspoon guar gum

Frosting

175g (7oz) white
chocolate, broken into
pieces

2 tablespoons milk

210ml (7floz) double
cream

To decorate

Raspberries, strawberries
and redcurrants

Preheat the oven to Gas Mark 5/190°C/375°F. Grease a heart-shaped baking tin (20cm/8in when measured across the widest part of the heart) and line the base with baking parchment. Alternatively, use mini heart moulds. This recipe makes twelve mini hearts like those in the photo.

With an electric mixer, cream the butter/margarine with the sugar until light and fluffy.

In a separate bowl, beat the eggs lightly.

Add the eggs a little at a time to the butter mixture. Beat between each addition until fully incorporated.

In a separate bowl, sieve the flours, baking powder and gum and stir until blended. There is no need to use an electric mixer – it can be done by hand.

Using a spoon, fold the flour into the egg mixture in three or four batches. Make sure it is all folded in before making the next addition.

If the mixture is too stiff and doesn't drop easily off a spoon, then add 1–2 teaspoons of warm water. Add one at a time and mix in to loosen the mixture.

Spread the mix in the tin and smooth it out.

Bake in a preheated oven on the centre shelf for about 25 minutes if making one large cake or 15 minutes if using the mini heart moulds. The sponge will be golden brown and springy when it is cooked.

Remove from the oven and leave to sit in the tin for 1–2 minutes before turning out onto a wire cooling tray. It is easier to do this if you loosen around the edges first with a knife.

Peel off the baking parchment and allow the cake to cool completely.

To finish

For the frosting, melt the chocolate with the milk in a heatproof bowl set over a saucepan of hot water over a medium heat. Remove from the heat and stir until smooth, then leave it to cool for 10 minutes. Whip the cream until it holds soft peaks and then fold it into the cooled chocolate mixture.

Spread the frosting over the top and sides of the cake, swirling with a palette knife.

Decorate with red fruit – raspberries, strawberries and redcurrants – and enjoy your St Valentine's Day!

Fresh yogurt cake with lime zest

I think that lime is very much an unsung hero, so I like to incorporate it into my recipes whenever I can.

For the cake

225g (9oz) Denise's
Delicious flour blend (p. 28)

1 teaspoon GF baking
powder

150ml (5floz) natural yogurt

135ml (4½floz) sunflower oil,
plus extra for greasing

225g (9oz) caster sugar

2 large eggs

Zest of 2 large limes, finely
grated

For the syrup

Juice of 2 large limes

65g (2½oz) caster sugar

2 tablespoons honey

25g (1oz) toasted flaked
almonds, to decorate

Preheat the oven to Gas Mark 5/190°C/375°F. Grease a 20cm/8in round cake tin with a removable base and line the base with baking parchment.

Mix the flour and baking powder.

Put the yogurt, oil, caster sugar, flour and baking powder mix, eggs and lime zest into a large bowl and beat together until smooth.

Turn the mixture into the prepared cake tin and bake on the centre shelf of the preheated oven for about 1 hour, until golden brown and a skewer inserted in the centre comes out clean.

Meanwhile, for the syrup, put the lime juice and caster sugar into a saucepan and heat gently until the sugar has dissolved. Bring to the boil, then simmer for 2–3 minutes. Stir in the honey.

When the cake is baked, carefully remove from the tin and place on a wire cooling rack set over a baking sheet. Prick the top of the cake all over with a fine skewer. If necessary, reheat the syrup, then pour the hot syrup over the warm cake and set aside to cool.

Scatter the flaked almonds on the top to decorate before serving. Serve warm with a scoop of vanilla ice cream.

Jewel cake

Don't forget to use Mum's trick of washing and drying the fruits and rolling them in ground almonds to make sure they rise in the cake.

100g (4oz) mixed coloured glacé cherries, halved, washed and dried

50g (2oz) stem ginger in syrup, chopped, washed and dried

50g (2oz) mixed peel, chopped

15g (½oz) ground almonds

50g (2oz) tapioca flour

75g (3oz) potato flour

75g (3oz) corn flour

1 teaspoon guar gum

1 teaspoon GF baking powder

150g (6oz) butter/margarine

150g (6oz) caster sugar

3 large eggs

Zest of 1 orange, finely grated

To decorate

150g (6oz) icing sugar, sieved

2–3 tablespoons freshly squeezed orange juice

50g (2oz) mixed coloured glacé cherries, chopped

25g (1oz) mixed peel, chopped

Preheat the oven to Gas Mark 5/190°C/375°F. Grease a 2lb/900g loaf tin and line the base and sides with baking parchment.

Place the cherries, stem ginger and mixed peel on a sheet of greaseproof paper and roll the fruits in the ground almonds until fully coated.

Sieve the flours, gum and baking powder into a separate bowl and mix well.

Place the butter/margarine and sugar in a mixing bowl and beat until light and fluffy. Beat in the eggs, one at a time. Fold in the flours with the orange zest, then stir in the dried fruit.

Transfer the cake mixture to the prepared tin and bake in the centre of the oven for about 1¼ hours, or until a skewer inserted into the centre of the cake comes out clean. Leave the cake to sit in the tin for about 5 minutes, then turn out onto a wire rack, peel off the baking parchment and leave to cool completely.

To decorate the cake, place the icing sugar in a mixing bowl. Stir in the orange juice and mix until smooth. Drizzle this icing over the cake. Mix together the chopped glacé cherries and mixed peel in a small bowl, then use to decorate the cake. Allow the icing to set before serving.

Apricot torte

When buying dried fruits, try to steer towards the fruits that are prepared without sulphites. In the case of apricots this means the ones that are a dull brown colour rather than a vivid orange.

90g (3½oz) natural dried apricots

Finely grated zest and juice of 1 large orange

150g (6oz) butter/margarine

150g (6oz) caster sugar

2 large eggs, separated

200g (8oz) fine ground polenta

90g (3½oz) ground almonds

1 teaspoon GF baking powder

Icing sugar to dust

Syrup

150ml (5floz) honey

100ml (3½floz) orange juice

2 teaspoons lemon juice

The night before making the cake, put the apricots, orange zest and juice in a bowl and soak overnight for 12 hours.

Preheat the oven to Gas Mark 5/190°C/375°F. Grease and line a 23cm/9in round loose-bottomed cake tin.

When ready to make the cake, transfer the apricots and juice to a food processor and blend until smooth.

Put the butter/margarine and sugar in a large bowl and beat together until light and fluffy. Add the egg yolks, one at a time, beating well after each addition.

In another bowl mix the polenta, ground almonds and baking powder. Add to the butter mixture and mix well. Fold in the apricot purée.

Whisk the eggs whites until stiff, then fold into the mixture. Turn the mixture into the prepared tin and bake in the centre of the preheated oven for about 45 minutes or until light golden brown and firm to the touch. Gently insert a skewer into the centre of the cake – it should come out dry.

Meanwhile, make the syrup. Put all the ingredients in a saucepan, bring to the boil, then simmer for 2–3 minutes until combined. Set aside.

When the cake is baked, let it stand in the tin for 5 minutes, then transfer to a wire rack set over a sheet of greaseproof paper. Prick the top of the cake all over with a fine skewer. If the syrup seems very thick, then reheat it. Spoon the hot syrup over the warm cake and leave on the wire rack to cool.

To serve, dust with icing sugar.

Orange & almond cake

This recipe bakes one 23cm/9in cake. However, there is plenty of mixture mix to make two 13cm/5in cakes so you can make one to eat and pop the other in the freezer.

200g (8oz) butter/margarine, at room temperature

175g (7oz) caster sugar

3 medium eggs, lightly beaten

200g (8oz) ground almonds

Juice of 1 orange

100g (4oz) polenta

1 teaspoon GF baking powder

Pinch of salt

To serve

Whipped cream

Summer fruits (raspberries, strawberries, blueberries, etc.)

Preheat the oven to Gas Mark 3/165°C/325°F. Brush a 23cm/9in round cake tin with a little melted butter/margarine and flour the tin with potato flour. Cut out a round of baking parchment the size of the base of the tin and line the base with it.

In a large mixing bowl, beat the butter/margarine until pale and fluffy. Add the sugar and beat again until light and creamy.

Add the eggs, a little at a time, beating well between each addition. Fold in the ground almonds, orange juice, polenta, baking powder and salt.

Pour the mixture into the prepared tin and bake in the centre of the oven for about 50–60 minutes if cooking the large cake, or 40 minutes if cooking two smaller ones, until the top of the cake is a deep golden colour and a skewer inserted into the centre comes out clean.

When removed from the oven, leave to cool in the tin for 10 minutes before turning out onto a wire rack and removing the baking parchment.

Decorate by generously covering the top of the cake with whipped cream and piling fresh berries in the centre.

Upside-down nutty caramel cake

I really like the combination of nuts and toffee in this recipe and it's very easy to put together but looks like it took a lot of effort! Make sure to serve at room temperature so that the caramel is soft.

Caramel topping

40g (1½oz) butter/margarine

50g (2oz) demerara sugar

2 tablespoons cream

2 tablespoons chopped, unsalted, roasted macadamias

2 tablespoons chopped, unsalted, roasted pistachios

2 tablespoons chopped, unsalted, roasted walnuts

For the cake

125g (5oz) butter/margarine, chopped

200g (8oz) demerara sugar

3 large eggs

50g (2oz) tapioca flour

50g (2oz) potato flour

50g (2oz) corn flour

1 teaspoon GF baking powder

½ teaspoon xanthan gum

¼ teaspoon bread soda

25g (1oz) cocoa powder

100g (4oz) dark chocolate, melted

180ml (6floz) milk

Whipped cream, to serve

Preheat the oven to Gas Mark 3/165°C/325°F. Grease a deep 20cm/8in round cake tin and line the base with baking parchment. Use a loose bottomed tin if possible.

For the caramel, combine the butter/margarine, sugar and cream in a small saucepan and stir with a wooden spoon over a low heat, without boiling, until the sugar is dissolved. Then, still stirring, bring to the boil and remove from the heat.

Pour the hot caramel over the base of the prepared tin, sprinkle the combined nuts over the caramel and pop into the freezer while preparing the cake mixture.

Beat the butter/margarine and sugar in a medium-sized bowl with an electric mixer until light and fluffy. Beat in the eggs, one at a time, until just combined between each addition.

Sieve the flours, baking powder, gum and bread soda to combine. Then sieve the cocoa powder into the flours. Sieve all the dry ingredients together three times to make sure the cocoa blends fully without any lumps.

Stir the dry ingredients into the butter mixture and mix well. Then add the melted chocolate and milk and mix again. Spread the cake mixture over the caramel nut topping.

Bake in the oven for about 1 hour and 10 minutes. Insert a skewer to ensure it is fully baked. Stand the cake in the tin for 15 minutes, before turning out onto a wire rack to cool.

Serve with some lightly whipped cream.

Blueberry & ricotta loaf

This is an unusual combination with a great cheese that doesn't get enough attention.

225g (9oz) Denise's Delicious flour blend (p. 28)

2 teaspoons GF baking powder

½ teaspoon xanthan gum

½ teaspoon salt

125g (5oz) blueberries

15g (½oz) ground almonds

150g (6oz) butter/margarine

200g (8oz) ricotta cheese

260g (10½oz) sugar

3 large eggs, lightly beaten

1 teaspoon vanilla extract

Preheat the oven to Gas Mark 4/180°C/350°F. Prepare a 1lb/450g loaf tin, greasing it well with butter/margarine and lining it with baking parchment or a ready-made liner.

In a medium-sized bowl, mix together the flour, baking powder, gum and salt.

Rinse the blueberries and toss them in the ground almonds to coat them lightly.

Using an electric mixer, beat together the butter/margarine, ricotta and sugar on a high speed for 3 minutes until pale and fluffy. Add the eggs one at a time, mixing on a medium speed after each addition until blended with the mixture. Mix in the vanilla extract.

Remove the bowl from the mixer and stir in the dry ingredients in three or four batches with a metal spoon until just incorporated. Do not over mix. Stir in the blueberries gently, trying not to crush them.

Pour the batter into the prepared tin, smoothing out the top with a spatula. Place in the centre of the oven. Bake for 1 hour 10 minutes–1 hour 20 minutes, or until a skewer comes out clean. If the cake seems very brown after 40 minutes, then cover it with a sheet of tinfoil to keep it from browning further.

Remove from the oven and let it cool for 15 minutes in the tin. Gently remove the cake from the tin and let it cool completely on a wire rack. Remove the parchment or baking liner before serving.

Tiramisu cake

The traditional biscuits used in tiramisu are not gluten-free, but that won't upset us gluten-free bakers!

Sponge

115g (4½oz) butter/margarine

2 teaspoons instant coffee powder

180ml (6floz) hot water

100g (4oz) dark chocolate, chopped

200g (8oz) caster sugar

100g (4oz) corn flour

75g (3oz) potato flour

1 teaspoon GF baking powder

½ teaspoon xanthan gum

2 tablespoons cocoa powder

1 large egg

1 teaspoon vanilla extract

Coffee syrup

390ml (13floz) water

100g (4oz) caster sugar

1 teaspoon instant coffee powder

2 tablespoons Marsala

Mascarpone topping

225g (9oz) mascarpone cheese

300ml (10floz) thick cream

120g (4½oz) raspberries

1 tablespoon cocoa powder

Preheat the oven to Gas Mark 4/180°C/350°F. Grease a 20cm/8in square cake tin and line the base with baking parchment.

Combine the butter/margarine, coffee powder, hot water, chocolate and sugar in a bain marie (a bowl over a saucepan of water) on a medium heat, and stir until the chocolate is melted. Place this chocolate mixture in large bowl and allow to cool for 5 minutes.

Sieve the flours, baking powder, gum and cocoa powder three times into a separate bowl to remove all the lumps from the cocoa powder.

Whisk the sieved flours and cocoa powder into the chocolate mixture in two batches. Then whisk in the egg and vanilla extract and pour the mixture into the prepared tin.

Bake for about 40 minutes until an inserted skewer comes out clean. Stand the cake in the tin for 5 minutes, before turning onto a wire rack to cool.

Coffee syrup

Meanwhile, combine the water, sugar and coffee for the syrup in a medium saucepan. Stir over a gentle heat until the sugar is dissolved. Then bring to the boil and boil uncovered, without stirring for 5 minutes. Remove from the heat, stir in the Marsala and allow to cool. Reserve a third of the coffee syrup for the mascarpone topping.

When the cake is cool, split it in half horizontally. Place the halves, crust-side up, on a tray; brush with the remaining coffee syrup. Cover and refrigerate for 3 hours at least.

Mascarpone topping

Cut each cake half into eight pieces separately, so that you have sixteen chunks in total. Combine the mascarpone, cream and reserved coffee syrup in a medium-sized bowl and whisk gently until the mixture thickens slightly.

Assemble the tiramisu in eight individual serving dishes: place a piece of cake in each dish, with a layer of mascarpone mixture on top, then another layer of cake and mascarpone. Finish with raspberries and dust with sieved cocoa powder. Tah dah!

Chapter 4

Biscuits and Cookies

Amaretti biscuits

Amaretti are naturally gluten-free. They keep really well in an airtight tin and are wonderful to nibble alongside a good cup of coffee. As crushed biscuit they make a wonderful base for cheesecakes and add a nutty note.

Makes 12–16

2 large egg whites

115g (4½oz) ground almonds

200g (8oz) caster sugar

¼ teaspoon almond essence

50g (2oz) crushed flaked almonds

Line two medium-sized baking trays with baking parchment.

Combine all the ingredients, except the crushed flaked almonds, and beat with a hand-held electric mixer for 3 minutes until fully mixed.

Allow to stand for 5 minutes.

Spoon the mixture into a piping bag with a 1cm/0.4in plain nozzle.

Pipe circles of 5cm/2in in diameter onto the lined baking trays.

Sprinkle each biscuit with crushed almonds.

Cover the trays loosely with a layer of baking parchment and leave overnight in a cool room.

Preheat the oven to Gas Mark 4/180°C/350°F. Bake the biscuits in the centre of the oven until golden brown. Allow them to cool for a few minutes on the tray before removing to a wire cooling rack.

Once fully cold, store in an airtight container.

Tip
These biscuits need to rest overnight before baking, so start a day before you actually want to have them ready!

Greek almond biscuits

These Greek biscuits are somewhat similar to their Italian cousins, amaretti. However, amaretti must be prepared the day before and must be piped. If you are happier using your hands rather than a piping bag, this Greek recipe may suit you better.

Makes 20–25

325g (13oz) ground almonds

200g (8oz) caster sugar

¼ teaspoon almond essence

3 large egg whites

75g (3oz) flaked almonds

Preheat the oven to Gas Mark 4/180°C/350°F. Grease a baking tray lightly and line with a sheet of baking parchment.

Combine the ground almonds, sugar and almond essence in a large bowl. Beat the egg whites lightly with an electric mixer and add to the almond mixture. Stir in with a metal spoon until the mixture forms a firm paste.

Place the flaked almonds on a tray. Taking a tablespoon of mix at a time, roll it into a log shape using your hands, then roll it in the flaked almonds, covering all sides.

Place each log on the prepared tray and curve them with your fingers to make crescent moon shapes.

Bake in the preheated oven for 15 minutes or until browned. When cooked, place on a wire rack to cool.

Store in an airtight container.

Banana & oat biscuits

In case you didn't know, cookies start their journey soft and chewy and go hard when stale. Biscuits should snap when fresh and go soft when stale! All like to be kept in an airtight container and to be eaten shortly after baking. Do check that your coeliac is happy to eat pure oats before serving.

Makes 10–12

75g (3oz) butter/margarine, softened

75g (3oz) caster sugar

1 small egg, beaten lightly

40g (1½oz) corn flour

40g (1½oz) potato flour

¼ teaspoon xanthan gum

¼ teaspoon bread soda

½ teaspoon salt

¼ teaspoon freshly grated nutmeg

¼ teaspoon ground cinnamon

1 banana, mashed

125g (5oz) pure oats

25g (1oz) hazelnuts, chopped finely

Line two baking trays with baking parchment, and preheat the oven to Gas Mark 5/190°C/375°F.

Put the butter/margarine and sugar in a large bowl and cream them together until light and fluffy with a hand-held electric mixer, then beat the egg into the mixture.

Sieve in the flours, gum, bread soda, salt and spices and mix on the lowest speed on your electric mixer.

Fold in the mashed banana, oats and hazelnuts, and mix well.

Drop heaped teaspoons of the mixture onto the prepared baking sheets, allowing about 5cm/2ins of space between each biscuit as the mixture will spread.

Bake in the oven for about 15 minutes, then transfer quickly to a wire rack and leave to cool. Once the biscuits are cool, pop into an airtight container to store.

Italian-style lemon & pistachio biscotti

Do use a good quality vanilla extract here – there's no match for the complex notes of good vanilla. These biscotti are a gorgeous treat with an afternoon espresso. They keep really well in an airtight container for several weeks.

Makes 20

50g (2oz) butter/margarine

200g (8oz) caster sugar

1 teaspoon vanilla extract

1 tablespoon grated lemon zest

4 medium eggs

100g (4oz) potato flour

100g (4oz) corn flour

90g (3½oz) rice flour

15g (½oz) chestnut flour

1 teaspoon guar gum

½ teaspoon bread soda

1 teaspoon GF baking powder

125g (5oz) unsalted shelled pistachios, chopped coarsely

2 tablespoons extra caster sugar, for sprinkling.

Preheat the oven to Gas Mark 4/180°C/350°F. Lightly grease a baking tray.

Beat the butter/margarine, sugar, vanilla extract and lemon zest in a medium-sized bowl until just combined. Beat three of the eggs in a separate jug and add one at a time, beating between additions until combined.

Sieve the flours, gum, bread soda and baking powder into a separate bowl. Then stir in the nuts. Add the flour mixture to the butter mixture and combine with an electric mixer on speed one. Only mix until combined, do not overbeat. Cover and refrigerate for 1 hour.

Knead the dough on a lightly floured surface, using potato flour, until smooth but still sticky. Halve the dough and shape each half into a 30cm/12in log. Place each log on the baking tray.

Combine the remaining egg with 1 tablespoon of water in a small bowl. Brush the egg mixture over the logs and sprinkle thickly with the extra sugar.

Bake in the preheated oven for about 20 minutes or until lightly browned and firm, then stand for 10 minutes on the baking tray out of the oven.

Reduce the oven temperature to Gas Mark 3/165°C/325°F.

Using a sharp bread knife with serrated edge, cut the logs diagonally into ten slices. Place the slices back on the baking tray.

Bake in the oven for about 15 minutes or until dry and crisp, turning halfway through cooking. Remove and cool on wire racks.

Store in an airtight container.

Triple chocolate-chip cookies

This is an absolute classic recipe and should be in every baker's repertoire.

Makes 12–15

100g (4oz) soft brown sugar

100g (4oz) caster sugar

100g (4oz) butter/margarine, softened

1 large egg

1 teaspoon vanilla extract

50g (2oz) tapioca flour

75g (3oz) potato flour

75g (3oz) corn flour

½ teaspoon GF baking powder

½ teaspoon guar gum

125g (5oz) milk chocolate, melted

75g (3oz) white chocolate, chips or chopped into chunks

75g (3oz) dark chocolate, chips or chopped into chunks

Heat the oven to Gas Mark 5/190°C/375°F. Line 1–2 baking trays with baking parchment.

Mix the sugars together in a medium-sized bowl, then cream with the butter/margarine.

Beat the egg in a separate bowl and add the vanilla extract. Add the egg to the butter mixture gradually, stirring between each addition.

In another bowl, sieve the flours, baking powder and gum.

Add the flour to the egg mixture and fold in.

Stir in half of the melted chocolate and add the chocolate chips/chunks and mix together.

Then use an ice-cream scoop or round tablespoon measure to scoop out balls of cookie dough and drop them straight onto the prepared trays.

Bake (in batches if necessary) for 8–9 minutes until pale golden and still soft to the touch, but the edges should be browned. They will firm up as they cool.

Carefully transfer to a wire rack as soon as they can be lifted up, then drizzle with the remaining melted chocolate and set aside to cool.

Store in an airtight container.

Chocolate-drizzled coconut biscuits

This is an all-in-one recipe, so a great one when you are caught for time.

....

Makes approximately 18

....

25g (1oz) rice flour

50g (2oz) potato flour

75g (3oz) corn flour

½ teaspoon xanthan gum

½ teaspoon GF baking powder

150g (6oz) butter/margarine, softened

100g (4oz) caster sugar

50g (2oz) desiccated coconut

Melted chocolate to decorate

Preheat the oven to Gas Mark 5/190°C/375°F and line two baking sheets with baking parchment.

Blend the flours, then add the gum and baking powder and mix well.

Using an electric mixer add the butter/margarine, sugar and coconut and beat until they combine to form a dough.

Knead the dough briefly, then break off even-sized balls about the size of marbles. Roll them (if the mixture is sticky dip your hands into potato flour before rolling) to a smooth shape in the palms of your hands. Place on the baking sheets and make sure to place them well spaced apart. Alternatively you can use a cookie cutter to make whatever shapes you fancy, as in the photo.

Bake in batches in the oven for 10–12 minutes or until flecked golden. Leave the biscuits to cool and harden slightly on the baking sheets for about 1 minute, then transfer to a wire rack and leave to cool completely. When cool, drizzle with the melted chocolate.

Make sure to store in an airtight container to keep the biscuits fresh, that is if they last that long!

Chocolate-chip & pecan cookies

This is a great base cookie recipe and the condensed milk helps to make a lovely, gooey, chewy cookie. You can substitute the chocolate and nuts with fruit of your choice.

Makes 18–20

150g (6oz) butter/margarine

75g (3oz) caster sugar

225g (9oz) Denise's Delicious flour blend (p. 28)

2 teaspoons GF baking powder

¼ teaspoon guar gum

90ml (3floz) condensed milk

75g (3oz) milk chocolate chips

40g (1½oz) unsalted, chopped pecan nuts

Preheat the oven to Gas Mark 5/190°C/375°F. Grease a baking tray lightly and cover with baking parchment.

Cream the butter/margarine and sugar in a medium-sized bowl using an electric mixer.

Sieve the flour, baking powder and gum in another bowl and set aside.

Add the condensed milk to the butter mixture and mix well.

Gradually add the dry ingredients to the butter mixture and combine.

Stir in the chocolate chips and the nuts.

Using an ice cream scoop, spoon the mix out onto the baking tray, leaving plenty of space between the cookies to allow them to spread.

Bake for 10–15 minutes until golden brown.

Remove from the oven and allow to cool on the tray for 5 minutes before removing to a wire cooling tray.

Store in an airtight container.

Chocolate peppermint cookies

These cookies are a fun way to celebrate St Patrick's Day. If you have a shamrock-shaped cutter, even better! Store the cookies in an airtight container until you are ready and add the frosting just before serving.

Makes 12–14

200g (8oz) Denise's Delicious flour blend (p. 28)

¼ teaspoon GF baking powder

2 tablespoons cocoa powder

¼ teaspoon salt

100g (4oz) butter/margarine, at room temperature

100g (4oz) caster sugar

1 large egg

½ teaspoon vanilla extract

For the frosting

200g (8oz) icing sugar

1 teaspoon peppermint extract

2–3 teaspoons water

Natural green food colouring

Preheat the oven to Gas Mark 5/190°C/375°F. Grease a baking tray lightly and place a sheet of baking parchment on top.

In a medium-sized bowl, sieve together the flour, baking powder, cocoa powder and salt. Sieve these three times to make sure the cocoa is blended.

In a large bowl, cream together the butter/margarine and sugar until light in colour and fluffy in texture. Beat in the egg and vanilla extract until combined, but do not overbeat. Add the dry ingredients and mix until the dough comes together and no streaks of dry ingredients remain.

Transfer the dough to a large sheet of baking parchment and shape into a log 4–5cm/1½–2in in diameter. Roll up in the parchment, wrapping well, and refrigerate for at least 2 hours, until firm.

Slice the chilled cookie dough log into rounds no more than ½cm/¼in thick. Alternatively, if you want to use a cookie cutter roll out the dough using some potato flour to stop it sticking and cut with a cookie cutter. Arrange on the prepared baking sheet leaving plenty of space between each cookie.

Bake for 11–13 minutes, until the cookies are set around the edges and firm.

Allow to cool on the baking sheet for 2–3 minutes, then transfer to a wire rack to cool completely before frosting.

To make the frosting

Sieve the icing sugar and whisk together with the other ingredients in a small bowl, adding enough green food colouring to make the frosting a bright green.

Add an additional teaspoon of water as needed to thin the icing if it becomes too thick. The icing should be thick enough to hold its shape.

Spoon on top of the cookies, whilst keeping them on the wire tray, in case any frosting drizzles off. Set aside to allow to set.

Cranberry & orange shortbread cookies

A nice light fruity biscuit.

Makes 12–16

100g (4oz) corn flour

100g (4oz) rice flour

75g (3oz) caster sugar

100g (4oz) butter/margarine, chilled and cut into small cubes

Juice of 1 small orange

50g (2oz) dried cranberries

Corn flour, for rolling out

Oil for greasing

Icing sugar to decorate

Preheat the oven to Gas Mark 5/190°C/375°F. Grease a baking tray.

Place the flours and sugar in a medium-sized bowl and, with an electric mixer, blend well. Add the cubed butter/margarine and mix until you have fine breadcrumbs.

Add the orange juice and cranberries to the mixing bowl and fold in.

Turn out and knead together well. Roll out quickly and evenly – if the dough is sticky, use a little corn flour on the board and on the dough.

Using a 6cm/2½in round biscuit cutter, cut out the biscuits and place well apart on the baking tray. Bake for 10–12 minutes, then cool on the baking tray before carefully lifting off.

Dust well with icing sugar to serve.

Lemon & lime bars

A zesty, citrus pick-me-up with a mid-morning cup of tea!

Makes 12–15

250g (10oz) Denise's Delicious flour blend (p. 28)

½ teaspoon xanthan gum

½ teaspoon GF baking powder

200g (8oz) butter/margarine, softened and cubed

100g (4oz) caster sugar

Zest of 1 large lemon, finely grated

Topping

2 large eggs

125g (5oz) caster sugar

Juice of ½ lemon

Juice of 1 lime

25g (1oz) tapioca flour

½ teaspoon xanthan gum

Icing sugar to dust

Preheat the oven to Gas Mark 5/190°C/375°F. Grease and line a 25cm x 30cm/10 x 12in Swiss roll tin with baking parchment, running the parchment up the sides of the tin.

Sieve the flour, gum and baking powder into a large bowl.

Add the butter/margarine, sugar and lemon zest and combine using an electric mixer on a medium speed.

Roll out the biscuit base using a little potato flour and press into the base of the tin.

Prick all over with a fork.

Bake in the oven for 10–12 minutes until golden brown.

Topping

In a medium-sized bowl, whisk the eggs and sugar thoroughly together. Add the lemon juice and lime juice and mix.

Separately, sieve the tapioca flour and gum. Add this to the egg mixture and beat well.

Pass the mixture through a fine sieve into a jug. Pour the mix over the biscuit base.

Carefully place in the centre of the preheated oven and cook for about 15 minutes or until just set – the topping should have a slight wobble!

Once cooked, remove from the oven and allow to cool completely in the tin. Once cooled, cut into bars and dust with icing sugar to serve.

French macaroons

Did you know that the colours of French macaroons were based on the colours of the dresses of Marie Antoinette's ladies-in-waiting? All those beautiful pastel shades! I've used red food colouring here to make lovely pink macaroons, but you can use whatever colouring you like, or for chocolate macaroons use cocoa powder.

Makes approximately 12

175g (7oz) icing sugar

115g (4½oz) ground almonds

3 large egg whites

2 tablespoons caster sugar

1–2 drops red natural food colouring

Filling

100g (4oz) icing sugar

100g (4oz) butter/margarine at room temperature, cubed

Juice and zest of 1 small lemon

Raspberry jam

Preheat the oven to Gas Mark ½/130°C/250°F. Lightly grease a large baking tray and line with baking parchment.

Sieve the icing sugar and combine with the ground almonds.

Whisk the egg whites, then add the caster sugar and continue to beat until stiff. Pour the ground almond mixture onto the whisked egg whites and mix with a spatula. Add the food colouring and mix well.

Pipe small discs, using a 1½cm/¾in plain nozzle, onto the prepared tray with plenty of space between them. Tap the trays on the countertop to allow the mixture to spread.

Leave to stand for 20 minutes before baking.

Bake in the centre of the oven for 20 minutes and cool for 5 minutes before removing to a wire tray. To remove the macaroons, slide a pallet knife underneath and gently transfer to the tray.

Filling

Sieve the icing sugar and then beat it together with the butter/margarine. Add the lemon juice and zest and mix.

Sandwich the macaroons together with a little jam and the buttercream and serve.

French-style honey madeleines

To make these properly you need to have the correct madeleine baking trays which you can easily buy online or find in a speciality baking shop. I first went on the hunt for a French madeleine recipe after reading Marcel Proust's In Search of Lost Time, *where he wrote profusely about the wonders of a madeleine! They are simple to make and live up to expectations.*

Makes 24

115g (4½oz) butter/margarine

100g (4oz) caster sugar

3 large eggs

50g (2oz) tapioca flour

50g (2oz) corn flour

25g (1oz) potato flour

1 teaspoon GF baking powder

½ teaspoon guar gum

1 heaped teaspoon honey

Juice of 1 lemon

Preheat the oven to Gas Mark 4/180°C/350°F. Grease two madeleine tins, with twelve shell-shaped moulds in each tin, thoroughly.

Cream the butter/margarine and sugar in a medium-sized bowl, using an electric mixer.

Beat in the eggs one at a time, mixing well between each addition.

Sieve the flours, baking powder and gum and fold into the butter mixture with a metal spoon.

Add the honey and lemon juice and fold in, making sure the honey is mixed through.

Place the tins on a baking tray and then carefully spoon in the mixture to three-quarter fill the moulds. Bake on the centre shelf of your oven for 6–7 minutes until golden brown and turn out of the tins immediately.

Allow to cool slightly on a wire rack and serve warm with a strong coffee.

After-dinner Florentines

Florentines are the best way to finish off a heavy meal, with a very strong coffee, although I do cheat sometimes and have them as a morning snack with a glass of milk. Don't let the reshaping step put you off. These taste so good, that misshapen Florentines will be forgiven!

Makes 10–12

75g (3oz) butter/ margarine

100g (4oz) caster sugar

50g (2oz) ground almonds

50g (2oz) mix of flaked almonds and chopped hazelnuts

50g (2oz) sultanas

Finely grated zest of 1 orange

1 tablespoon double cream

100g (4oz) dark or milk chocolate (whichever you prefer), broken into pieces

Line a baking tray with baking parchment. Preheat the oven to Gas Mark 2/150°C/300°F.

Put the butter/margarine and sugar in a saucepan and heat gently, stirring until completely dissolved. Remove from the heat and stir in all the remaining ingredients, except the cream and chocolate. Leave to cool slightly, then stir in the cream.

Place the mixture on the lined baking sheet, a dessert-spoon at a time, allowing room for spreading. Bake for 10 minutes.

Take the tray out of the oven. At this stage the biscuits will have spread unevenly and the mixture is pliable. It is akin to molten lava, so take care of your fingers! Using a knife or biscuit cutter, pull the biscuits roughly back into a circular shape.

Return the baking tray to the oven for 2–3 minutes to finish baking, then remove again. Leave the Florentines on the baking tray for 2–3 minutes before attempting to remove them. To remove, slide a palette knife underneath each biscuit (they will be starting to harden by now) and transfer them to a wire rack.

When the biscuits are cold and crisp, turn them face down. Put the chocolate in a heatproof bowl set over a pan of simmering water and stir until the chocolate has melted. Coat the backs of the Florentines with the melted chocolate and score with a fork or press with a rippled stamp (as I have done in our photo) to finish off.

Leave to set for about 30 minutes.

When completely cold, store in an airtight container, interleaving them with greaseproof paper so that they don't stick together.

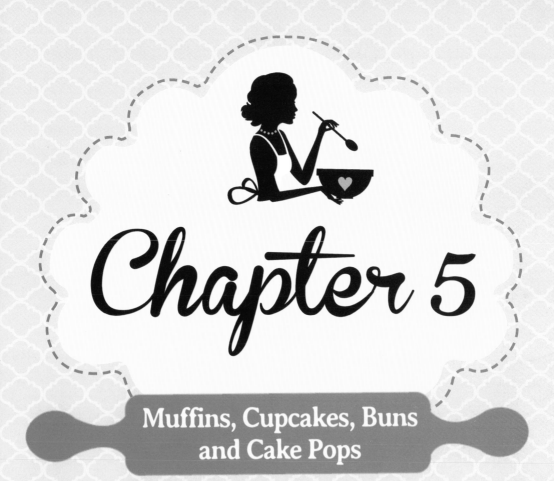

Chapter 5

Muffins, Cupcakes, Buns and Cake Pops

Chocolate-chip muffins

This is a different method to the other muffin recipes in this book but the same golden rule applies: do not over mix and prepare these by hand, never with an electric mixer.

Makes 12

225g (9oz) Denise's Delicious flour blend (p. 28)

Pinch of salt

½ teaspoon xanthan gum

1 teaspoon GF baking powder

75g (3oz) caster sugar

75g (3oz) butter/margarine at room temperature

75g (3oz) dark chocolate, finely chopped

1 large egg

180ml (6floz) single cream (approx.)

Chocolate chips to decorate

Preheat the oven to Gas Mark 5/190°C/375°F. Line a twelve-hole muffin tin with muffin cases.

Sieve the flour, salt, gum, baking powder and sugar into a mixing bowl. Add the butter/margarine and, using the tips of your fingers, rub in until the mixture resembles fine breadcrumbs.

Stir in the chocolate.

Break the egg into a measuring jug and then add enough cream to make the total liquid 230ml/7½floz. Stir to combine. Add the egg mixture to the other ingredients and mix gently with a metal spoon until the dough comes together – it will be quite sticky.

Gently divide the dough equally between the pre-pared muffin cases, then decorate with chocolate chips.

Bake in the oven for 10 minutes, then reduce the heat to Gas Mark 4/180°C/350°F and bake for a further 5–10 minutes or until firm to the touch. If a skewer is inserted into the centre, it should come out dry.

Remove from the oven and remove from the baking tin after 2–3 minutes. Allow to cool on a wire rack. When completely cool, store in an airtight container.

Banana muffins

This recipe is a great way to disguise fruit and ensures that the kids eat bananas without realising it. Also you can now buy really cute muffin cases that also persuade the smallies that muffins are worth a try!

Makes 12

150g (6oz) sugar

¼ teaspoon salt

1 teaspoon GF baking powder

15g (½oz) teff flour

50g (2oz) potato flour

50g (2oz) tapioca flour

65g (2½oz) corn flour

½ teaspoon guar gum

1 teaspoon cinnamon

2 large eggs

1 teaspoon vanilla extract

75g (3oz) butter/margarine, melted and cooled

3–4 ripe bananas, mashed

Preheat the oven to Gas Mark 5/190°C/375°F. Line a twelve-hole muffin tin with muffin cases.

Combine the sugar, salt, baking powder, flours, gum and cinnamon in a bowl and mix well.

In a measuring jug, beat together the eggs, vanilla extract and cooled, melted butter/margarine.

Pour the wet ingredients into the dry and, using a wooden spoon, mix gently to combine. Do not beat the mixture.

Fold in the mashed bananas, stirring gently.

Spoon into the muffin cases and bake for 20 minutes, by which time the muffins should be risen and golden and firm on top. If a skewer is inserted into the centre, it should come out dry.

Remove from the oven and remove from the baking tin after 2–3 minutes. Allow to cool on a wire rack. When completely cool, store in an airtight container.

Very berry muffins

The secret to a good muffin is not to overbeat them. Never, ever mix with an electric beater. Gently fold in the mixture by hand. This mix is loaded with fruit for a fabulous burst of flavour! This recipe makes 8 generous muffins or 12 smaller ones.

Makes 12

200g (8oz) Denise's Delicious flour blend (p. 28)

½ teaspoon bread soda

2 teaspoons GF baking powder

1 teaspoon guar gum

75g (3oz) caster sugar

Pinch of salt

210ml (7floz) buttermilk

1 large egg

75g (3oz) butter/margarine, melted and cooled

175g (7oz) soft fruits: raspberry, strawberries and blueberries

Preheat the oven to Gas Mark 5/190°C/375°F. Line a twelve-hole muffin tin with muffin cases.

Combine the flour, bread soda, baking powder, gum, salt and sugar in a bowl and mix well.

In a measuring jug, beat together the buttermilk, egg and melted butter/margarine.

Using a wooden spoon, stir the buttermilk mixture into the flour mixture and mix gently to combine. Do not beat the mixture.

Fold in the berries, stirring gently.

Spoon into the muffin cases and bake for 20 minutes, by which time the muffins should be risen and golden and firm on top. If a skewer is inserted into the centre, it should come out dry.

Remove from the oven and remove from the baking tin after 2–3 minutes. Allow to cool on a wire rack. When completely cool, store in an airtight container.

St Patrick's Day green velvet cupcakes

What can I say; a tasty St Patrick's Day treat!

Makes 12

75g (3oz) tapioca flour

15g (½oz) teff flour

115g (4½oz) corn flour

125g (5oz) potato flour

¼ teaspoon salt

4 teaspoons GF baking powder

¾ teaspoon guar gum

200g (8oz) butter/margarine, at room temperature

300g (12oz) caster sugar

3 large eggs

2½ teaspoons vanilla extract

390ml (13floz) warm milk

To decorate

150g (6oz) butter/margarine at room temperature

300g (12oz) icing sugar, sieved

½ teaspoon vanilla extract

Natural green food colouring

Melted dark chocolate

Preheat the oven to Gas Mark 5/190°C/375°F. Line a twelve-hole queen cake tin with paper cases.

Sieve together the flours, salt, baking powder and gum and set aside.

Cream the butter/margarine and sugar with a hand-held mixer until light and fluffy.

In a small bowl, beat the eggs lightly with the vanilla extract and add to the butter mixture gradually, beating between each addition.

Add the flour mixture three tablespoons at a time, folding in between each addition.

Add the milk to the bowl, mixing thoroughly.

Divide the mixture evenly between the paper cases.

Bake in the centre of a preheated oven until golden brown and an inserted skewer comes out dry. Remove from the oven and cool on a wire rack.

To decorate

Cut the butter/margarine into small cubes and place in a medium-sized bowl with the icing sugar. Mix with a hand-held electric mixer until fully blended. Add the vanilla extract and beat again.

Add 4–5 drops of green colouring to the bowl. Stir in well until you achieve a bright green colour.

Fill a piping bag with the green buttercream and, using a wide star nozzle, pipe onto the cupcakes in nice high spirals.

Top off with a drizzle of melted chocolate and allow the chocolate to cool before serving.

Easter cupcakes

Whilst any madeira mixture works for cupcakes, this recipe is great because the cakes bake with a flat top, which makes it easier for you to get creative with your piping skills.

Makes 12

75g (3oz) tapioca flour

15g (½oz) teff flour

115g (4½oz) corn flour

125g (5oz) potato flour

¼ teaspoon salt

4 teaspoons GF baking powder

¾ teaspoon guar gum

200g (8oz) butter/margarine, at room temperature

300g (12oz) caster sugar

3 large eggs

1½ teaspoons vanilla extract

390ml (13floz) warm milk

To decorate

150g (6oz) butter/margarine at room temperature

300g (12oz) icing sugar, sieved

½ teaspoon vanilla extract

Red and green natural food colouring

12 fluffy Easter chicks or mini chocolate eggs (make sure they are gluten free please!)

Preheat the oven to Gas Mark 5/190°C/375°F. Line a twelve-hole queen cake tin with paper cases.

Sieve together the flours, salt, baking powder and gum and set aside.

Cream the butter/margarine and sugar with a hand-held electric mixer until light and fluffy.

In a small bowl, beat the eggs lightly with the vanilla extract and add to the butter mixture gradually, beating between each addition.

Add the flour mixture three tablespoons at a time and fold in between each addition.

Add the milk to the bowl, mixing thoroughly.

Divide the mixture evenly between the paper cases.

Bake in the centre of the preheated oven until golden brown and an inserted skewer comes out dry. Remove from the oven and cool on a wire rack.

To decorate

Cut the butter/margarine into small cubes and place in medium-sized bowl with the icing sugar. Mix with an electric hand-held mixer until fully blended. Add the vanilla extract and beat again.

Divide the mixture between two bowls, adding 2–3 drops of red food colouring to the first bowl and green colouring to the second bowl. Stir them well until you achieve a pale pink and pale green colour.

Fill a piping bag with pale pink buttercream and pipe onto half of the cupcakes using a wide star nozzle.

Use a circular motion to build the buttercream into a spiral.

With a second piping bag and the same size nozzle, repeat this step with the green icing on the remainder of the cakes.

Finish off the cakes with Easter decorations such as fluffy yellow chicks or gluten-free mini chocolate eggs.

Pecan & praline cupcakes

This is a very grown-up cupcake. No need to pipe on buttercream here if you haven't time, a dollop will suffice nicely. The praline can be made in advance and a sprinkle will liven up any cake. However, if you do not have time to make the praline, fear not. An alternative way to finish the cupcakes is to sprinkle some crushed nuts on top.

Makes 12

75g (3oz) tapioca flour

15g (½oz) teff flour

115g (4½oz) corn flour

125g (5oz) potato flour

¼ teaspoon salt

4 teaspoons GF baking powder

¾ teaspoon guar gum

200g (8oz) butter/margarine, at room temperature

300g (12oz) caster sugar

3 large eggs

2½ teaspoons vanilla extract

50g (2oz) pecan nuts, chopped

390ml (13floz) warm milk

Vanilla buttercream to decorate

150g (6oz) butter/margarine

300g (12oz) icing sugar, sieved

½ teaspoon vanilla extract

Praline

100g (4oz) roughly chopped mixed nuts (blanched almonds, peeled hazelnuts, pecan nuts)

125g (5oz) sugar

Preheat the oven to Gas Mark 5/190°C/375°F. Line a twelve-hole queen cake tin with paper cases.

Sieve together the flours, salt, baking powder and gum and set aside.

Cream the butter/margarine and sugar until light and fluffy with a hand-held electric mixer.

In a small bowl, beat the eggs lightly with the vanilla extract and add to the butter mixture gradually, beating between each addition.

Add the flour mixture three tablespoons at a time and fold in between each addition.

Add the pecan nuts and mix in.

Add the milk, mixing thoroughly.

Divide the mixture evenly between the paper cases.

Bake in the centre of the preheated oven until golden brown and an inserted skewer comes out dry. Remove from the oven and cool on a wire rack.

Vanilla buttercream

Cut the butter/margarine into small cubes and place in a medium-sized bowl with the icing sugar. Mix with a hand-held electric mixer until fully blended. Add the vanilla extract and beat again.

Spread a dollop of the vanilla buttercream on top of each cupcake, or, if you have time, fill a piping bag with the buttercream and, using a wide star nozzle, pipe onto the cupcakes in nice high spirals.

Praline

Prepare a baking sheet by lightly oiling it and set aside.

Place the nuts on a baking tray and place under the grill for five minutes, until the skins blister and the almonds and hazelnuts turn golden brown.

Place the sugar in a heavy-bottomed pan and heat over a gentle heat without adding any liquid and stir continuously until it has melted completely and is a light golden colour.

Add the nuts and cook for one minute, stirring to allow the nuts to be fully coated. Pour the mixture onto the baking sheet and allow to cool at room temperature for approximately 20 minutes.

Then either break up in the food processor or beat with a rolling pin. When cool, store the praline in an airtight container at room temperature.

To finish the cupcakes, sprinkle them generously with praline.

Cranberry & sultana rock buns

This recipe brings me back to secondary school and early baking lessons with Sister Hilary! There's something very comforting about rock buns and they are a great success for lunch boxes and keep really well. When buying dried fruit, do be mindful of the level of sulphites that is used to preserve them. Try to find natural fruit with a low level of sulphites.

Makes 14–16

250g (10oz) Denise's Delicious flour blend (p. 28)

½ teaspoon GF baking powder

125g (5oz) butter/margarine, cut into cubes and softened

100g (4oz) demerara sugar

2 large eggs, beaten lightly

4 tablespoons milk (approx.)

40g (1½oz) dried cranberries

40g (1½oz) sultanas

Preheat the oven to Gas Mark 5/190°C/375°F and line two baking sheets with baking parchment.

Mix the flour and baking powder and sieve into a bowl.

Add the butter/margarine, sugar and eggs and beat together using an electric mixer on a slow speed until combined. Add the milk, one tablespoon at a time, as necessary, to give the mixture a dropping consistency, then stir in the dried fruits.

Using two forks or, better still, using your hands, form the mixture into small balls (if forming with your hands and the mixture feels very sticky, then dab some potato flour on your hands before moulding) and place the buns spaced well apart on the lined baking sheets.

Bake in the preheated oven for 20 minutes or until golden. The bottoms of the rock buns when lifted should be medium gold in colour.

Transfer to a wire rack and leave to cool completely before serving.

Butterfly buns

I have loved butterfly buns since I was a little girl; I can still scoff several in one sitting! I like to attack a wing at a time with a blob of cream and jam and then the bun itself. That way I have some hope of ending up without icing sugar and cream in my hair!

Makes 12

150g (6oz) Denise's Delicious flour blend (p. 28)

Pinch of salt

1 teaspoon guar gum

1 teaspoon GF baking powder

100g (4oz) butter/margarine, at room temperature

90g (3½oz) caster sugar

2 medium eggs

To decorate

240ml (8floz) whipping cream

Raspberry jam

Icing sugar to dust

Heat the oven to Gas Mark 5/190°C/375°F. Line a twelve-hole queen cake tin with paper cases.

Sieve the flour, salt, gum and baking powder into a medium-sized bowl.

In a mixing bowl, cream the butter/margarine and sugar together with an electric mixer until light and fluffy.

Lightly beat the eggs in another bowl, then add into the butter/margarine mixture gradually whilst beating on the lowest speed.

Mix in the dry ingredients, again on the lowest setting. Mix until the flour is combined but do not overbeat.

Divide the mixture evenly between the paper cases and bake in a preheated oven for 15–20 minutes until golden brown and a skewer comes out dry.

Cool on a wire rack.

To decorate

Whip the cream until it stays on the whisk. If it is too loose, it will run off the cakes, but if it is too tight it doesn't look well, although it won't affect the taste.

When the cakes are cold, cut a slice off the top of each and cut these slices in half. Using a teaspoon, put a generous blob of whipped cream on top of the cake, then place a small amount of jam in the centre of the cream.

Place the two halves of each round upright, cut side down, in the cream to resemble wings.

Dust lightly with icing sugar.

Cake pops

It goes without saying that these are a huge hit with the smallies! The sponge needs to be made the day before making the cake pops, so that it crumbles well. It won't crumble if it's too fresh.

Makes 20–24

Sponge

125g (5oz) butter/margarine at room temperature

100g (4oz) sugar

3 large eggs

115g (4½oz) Denise's Delicious flour blend (p. 28)

2 teaspoons GF baking powder

To make the pops

75g (3oz) mascarpone cheese

½ teaspoon vanilla or almond extract

65g (2½oz) icing sugar, sieved

To decorate

200g (8oz) milk chocolate, roughly chopped

24 lolly sticks

140g (5½oz) icing sugar, sieved

4 tablespoons cold water

A few drops of natural red food colouring

24 small gluten-free coloured sweets and sugar sprinkles to decorate

Sponge

Prepare the sponge the day before making the cake pops. Preheat the oven to Gas Mark 5/190°C/375°F. Grease and line two 18cm/7in round tins with baking parchment.

Cream the butter/margarine and sugar with an electric mixer until light and fluffy.

Add the eggs, one at a time, mixing well between each addition.

Sieve the flour and baking powder into a separate bowl.

Add the flour mixture to the butter mixture two tablespoons at a time, beating on a low setting between each addition until combined.

Divide between the two tins. Bake in the preheated oven for approximately 20 minutes until golden brown and a skewer comes out dry.

Remove to a wire rack to cool.

To make the pops

Line a baking tray with baking parchment and ensure you have enough mini paper cases.

Crumble the cold sponge cake into a mixing bowl. Add the mascarpone and vanilla or almond extract, sieve in the icing sugar and mix together until you have a thick paste.

Using your hands, roll a 25g (1oz) piece of the paste into a ball. If it is very sticky use a small amount of icing sugar on your hands. Push this ball into a mini paper case, pressing it down so that when it is removed from the case it is a mini cupcake shape.

Shape the remaining cake pops in the same way. Place on the baking tray and chill in the refrigerator for 1–2 hours.

To decorate

Put the chocolate in a heatproof bowl, set the bowl over a saucepan of gently simmering water and heat until melted. Remove from the heat.

Push a lolly stick into each cake pop and make sure it is secure, then remove the paper case. Dip into the chocolate, turning it until coated. Lift it from the bowl, letting the excess drip back into the bowl, then place it over a cup or tumbler and turn until the chocolate is beginning to set. If you allow them to sit on baking parchment while setting, the pops will have a flat side.

Put it down gently on some clean baking parchment and repeat with the remaining cake pops.

Chill in the fridge until the chocolate has set completely.

Mix the icing sugar with one tablespoon of water at a time until it forms a smooth paste. Beat in the red colouring, a drop at a time until the icing is pink.

Spoon a little onto a cake pop, twirling the pop in your hand until the icing covers the sides of the pop as well as the top.

Before the icing sets, place a small sweet on the centre of each cake pop and scatter with sugar sprinkles. Place these on a cake pop display to finish setting. If you haven't got a display you can improvise by taping a piece of Styrofoam to your work surface and pushing the sticks into this.

Chapter 6

Tarts and Tray Bakes

Strawberry tart with crème pâtissière

This is a real summertime treat!

1 quantity of sweet pastry
(p. 30)

6 large egg yolks

115g (4½oz) caster sugar

40g (1½oz) corn flour

510ml (17floz) milk

1 vanilla pod, split

Icing sugar, to dust

1 large punnet of
strawberries

1½–2 tablespoons apricot
jam

Make the pastry according to the instructions. While it is chilling, preheat the oven to Gas Mark 6/200°C/400°F.

Roll out the pastry on a board floured with a little potato flour. Grease a 20cm/8in pie plate very well, making sure all sides are well greased.

Lifting the rolled out pastry on a rolling pin, line the pie plate with it, tucking in gently and trimming any excess with a sharp knife.

Bake blind for about 15 minutes until the pastry is golden brown. There is no need to use baking beans when baking gluten-free pastry.

To make the crème pâtissière, place the egg yolks and about one-third of the sugar in a bowl and whisk until pale and forming a light ribbon when the whisk is lifted out of the mixture.

Sieve the corn flour and mix well into the egg and sugar mixture.

Combine the milk, the remaining sugar and the split vanilla pod in a saucepan and bring to the boil. As soon as the mixture bubbles, remove the vanilla pod and, with a sharp knife, scrape out the vanilla seeds and add to the milk mixture.

Pour about one-third of the milk mixture onto the egg mixture, whisking vigorously all the time. Pour this back into the pan with the rest of the milk and cook over a gentle heat, whisking continuously. Boil for 2 minutes, then pour the crème into a bowl.

Dust lightly with icing sugar and place a piece of greaseproof paper on top of it to prevent a skin from forming as the crème cools. If a skin does form it will adhere to the greaseproof paper and be easy to remove.

When the crème has cooled, remove the greaseproof paper and pour into the tart base, then smooth out evenly.

Wash and dry the strawberries and halve them, cutting off the stems.

Lay out the strawberries on top of the crème, arranging them as nicely as possible, trying not to leave any gaps.

Place the apricot jam in a microwaveable dish and microwave on full power for 10 seconds until warmed.

Beat the jam with a spoon.

Using a pastry brush, lightly brush the strawberries with the apricot jam to glaze and give a shiny finish.

Autumnal pumpkin pie

The first time I had pumpkin pie was at my friend Bronwyn's wedding in San Diego on Thanksgiving. Pumpkin pie is a traditional Thanksgiving dessert and I absolutely fell in love with it. Pumpkin in cans can be found more easily these days in specialist food shops, but buy plenty when you find it. Canned pumpkin does not usually have any other ingredients added. However, as always with gluten-free/wheat-free baking, check the ingredients list to be sure.

1 quantity of sweet pastry (p. 30)

425g (17oz) can of solid pack pumpkin

150g (6oz) caster sugar

1½ teaspoons mixed spice

240ml (8floz) evaporated milk

2 medium eggs, lightly beaten

Make the pastry according to the instructions. While it is chilling, preheat the oven to Gas Mark 6/200°C/400°F.

Roll out the pastry on a board floured with a little potato flour. Grease a 20cm/8in pie plate very well, making sure all sides are well greased.

Lifting the rolled out pastry on a rolling pin, line the pie plate with it, tucking in gently and trimming any excess with a sharp knife.

Bake blind for about 15 minutes until the pastry is golden brown. There is no need to use baking beans when baking gluten-free pastry. Allow to cool.

In a large mixing bowl, mix the contents of the pumpkin tin with a hand-held mixer.

Add the sugar, spice, evaporated milk and eggs and mix on a low speed. When fully combined, pour the mixture into the cooled pastry base.

Reduce the oven temperature to Gas Mark 4/180°C/350°F.

Bake for 40–50 minutes or until a knife inserted near the centre comes out clean.

Allow to cool before serving.

Fig & honey tart

Do try to use a local honey. You'll be supporting local cottage industries but it's also great for hay fever to eat local honey. We are very spoilt having Dad as our in-house beekeeper!

1 quantity sweet pastry (p. 30)

6 fresh green figs

50g (2oz) caster sugar

600ml (20floz) water

450g (1lb) mascarpone cheese

4 medium egg yolks

½ teaspoon vanilla extract

2 tablespoons honey, plus 1 teaspoon for drizzling

50g (2oz) icing sugar

Make the pastry according to the instructions. While it is chilling, preheat the oven to Gas Mark 6/200°C/400°F.

Roll out the pastry on a board floured with a little potato flour. Grease a 20cm/8in pie plate very well, making sure all sides are well greased.

Lifting the rolled out pastry on a rolling pin, line the pie plate with it, tucking in gently and trimming any excess with a sharp knife.

Bake blind for about 15 minutes until the pastry is golden brown. There is no need to use baking beans when baking gluten-free pastry. Remove the pastry case from the oven and turn it down to Gas Mark 5/190°C/375°F.

Put the figs, half the caster sugar and the water in a pan and bring to the boil. Poach gently for 10 minutes, drain and cool.

Stir together the mascarpone cheese, egg yolks and vanilla extract in a bowl, add the remaining caster sugar and two tablespoons of honey and mix well. Sieve in the icing sugar and mix again. Spoon into the tart case and bake for 30 minutes.

To serve, cut the figs in half lengthways and arrange on the tart, cut-side up. Drizzle with the extra honey and serve at once.

Hazelnut & raspberry tart

This is a nice pastry with hazelnuts and cocoa, and the raspberry filling gives a lovely light contrast.

200g (8oz) hazelnuts

100g (4oz) butter/margarine, at room temperature

100g (4oz) icing sugar, sieved, plus extra for sprinkling

3 large egg yolks

75g (3oz) corn flour

75g (3oz) potato flour

50g (2oz) tapioca flour

½ teaspoon GF baking powder

1 teaspoon xanthan gum

2 teaspoons ground cinnamon

½ teaspoon grated nutmeg

25g (1oz) cocoa powder

Raspberry filling

1½ tablespoons corn flour

3 tablespoons caster sugar, or to taste

600g (1lb 7oz) fresh raspberries

Preheat the oven to Gas Mark 5/190°C/375°F. Grease a 20cm/8in round pie dish well.

Put the hazelnuts into an ovenproof dish and toast for around 15 minutes or until light golden brown.

If the nuts still have their papery brown skin, put them in a clean, dry tea towel, then gather up the ends and rub the nuts together to loosen the skins.

Allow the skinned nuts to cool, then transfer them to a food processor and grind to a fine powder.

Put the butter/margarine into a mixing bowl and, using an electric mixer, beat until creamy. Add the icing sugar and beat, slowly at first, until light and fluffy. Add in the egg yolks, one at a time, beating well after each addition.

Sieve the flours, baking powder, gum and spices. Then add the cocoa powder and sieve three times with the flour to ensure the cocoa is fully blended into the flour. Add this to the butter mixture and finally add the ground nuts and work in, using your hands to bring the pastry together if it is too stiff for the mixer.

Take three-quarters of the pastry and roll it out between two pieces of cling film. Peel off the top layer of cling film and turn the pastry into the prepared pie dish. Use the remaining layer of cling film to press the pastry into the pie dish and mould it into the sides. Chill the pastry case for 15 minutes.

Roll the remaining pastry in the same way to a rectangle about 23cm x 14cm/9in x 5½in. Cut into strips about 1cm/½in wide.

Raspberry filling

Sprinkle the corn flour and sugar over the raspberries and toss gently until almost mixed. Transfer into the pastry case and spread gently and evenly over the base.

Arrange the pastry strips in a lattice over the filling. Bake in the oven for about 25–30 minutes, until the pastry is a slightly darker brown and just firm. Let it cool, then remove from the pan and serve sprinkled with icing sugar and accompanied by some hazelnut ice cream.

Luscious lime meringue tarts

To prevent curdling, always remember the golden rule: add hot liquids to cold – never cold to hot!

Makes 8

Meringue

3 large egg whites

½ teaspoon white vinegar

¼ teaspoon vanilla extract

¼ teaspoon salt

125g (5oz) caster sugar

Lime custard

75g (3oz) potato flour

150g (6oz) caster sugar

18ml (6floz) cold water

3 large egg yolks

5 tablespoons lime juice

1 tablespoon grated lime zest

2 tablespoons butter/margarine

To decorate

200ml whipped cream

1 teaspoon runny honey

Preheat the oven to Gas Mark 4/180°C/350°F. Line a baking tray with baking parchment.

Beat the egg whites, vinegar, vanilla extract and salt in a large bowl on a medium speed until soft peaks form.

Gradually beat in the sugar, one tablespoon at a time, on a high speed until stiff glossy peaks form and the sugar is blended.

Spoon the egg white mixture into eight mounds on the prepared tray. Flatten into cup shapes with a spoon.

Bake in the preheated oven for 35 minutes, then turn off the oven but leave the door closed to allow the shells to dry out in oven for at least 1 hour. Remove from the oven and remove the shells from the baking parchment.

Custard

In a small saucepan, combine the flour and sugar. Stir in the water until smooth. Whisk over a medium heat until thickened and bubbly. Reduce the heat and stir for an additional 2 minutes. Remove from the heat.

Whisk the egg yolks briefly. Stir a small amount of the hot mixture into the egg yolks and whisk quickly. Return this mixture to the pan and mix all together, whisking continuously. Bring to a gentle boil and stir for 2 minutes longer. Remove from the heat, then gently stir in the lime juice, zest and butter/margarine. Cool for 10 minutes without stirring.

Place a disc of greaseproof paper on top of the custard and set aside to chill in the fridge.

Just before serving, fill the meringue shells with the lime custard.

Combine the cream with the honey and mix well. Top each custard tart with a dollop of cream and serve.

Lemon curd tartlets

The tartness of the lemon cuts through the richness of the pastry here. One tartlet is plenty in one sitting! Alternatively, you can make bite-sized tartlets, as I have shown in the photo here, but one of those will not be enough, I guarantee!

Makes 8

1 quantity of sweet pastry (p. 30)

4 large eggs

200g (8oz) butter/margarine, at room temperature

300g (12oz) caster sugar

Zest and juice of 2 lemons

To serve

Fresh strawberries

Prepare the pastry according to the instructions. While it is chilling, preheat the oven to Gas Mark 6/200°C/400°F.

Prepare eight fluted 7½cm/3in tartlet dishes by greasing well. Alternatively you can use a larger quantity of little 'petit-four' style tartlet moulds.

Roll out the pastry on a board floured with a little potato flour.

Cut the pastry with a scone cutter to fit the tins, tucking the pastry in gently and trimming any excess with a sharp knife.

Bake blind for about 10 minutes (4 minutes if making the mini tartlets) until the pastry is golden brown. There is no need to use baking beans when baking gluten-free pastry.

Lemon curd

Place a pan of water on a medium heat. Sit a bowl into the pan that fits snugly.

Break the eggs into the bowl and whisk.

Cut the butter/margarine into small cubes and add gradually to the egg, whisking continuously.

Add the sugar, lemon juice and lemon zest and continue to whisk until the mixture thickens (see tip).

Take the bowl off the heat but continue to whisk until cooled.

Place a disc of greaseproof paper on top of the curd until needed.

To serve

Whip the cooled lemon curd lightly to ensure there are no lumps.

Spoon this into the pastry tartlets and chill in the fridge for 30 minutes.

Before serving, decorate with some fresh strawberries and dust with icing sugar if you like.

Tip

If your curd is not thickening (due to too much fruit juice), then add another egg yolk and beat in well whilst over the heat.

Gooseberry frangipane tartlets

Admittedly, topping and tailing gooseberries can be tedious but there's only a small amount here. Dad is a big fan of gooseberries and always says that they are the forgotten children of the fruit garden, so we're giving them their own recipe here to mark their importance!

Makes 8

1 quantity of sweet pastry (p. 30)

Icing sugar for dusting

Gooseberry filling

150g (6oz) gooseberries

100g (4oz) caster sugar (or more to taste)

2 tablespoons water

Frangipane

200g (8oz) butter/margarine

4 large eggs

175g (7oz) caster sugar

50g (2oz) tapioca flour

150g (6oz) ground almonds

50g (2oz) flaked almonds

Make the pastry according to the instructions. While it is chilling, preheat the oven to Gas Mark 5/190°C/375°F.

Grease eight fluted 7½cm/3in tartlet tins well.

Roll out the pastry on a board floured with a little potato flour.

Cut the pastry with a large scone cutter to fit the tins, tucking in gently and trimming any excess with a sharp knife. There is no need to bake the pastry blind for these tartlets.

Gooseberry filling

Place the topped and tailed gooseberries in a medium saucepan, with the sugar and water.

Poach the gooseberries over a gentle heat stirring occasionally. Do not bring to the boil, and watch over them as you want the fruits to soften without losing their shape. Taste to ensure that they are sweet enough for you, as gooseberries can be quite tart.

Set aside to cool.

Place a generous spoon of gooseberry filling into each tart base.

Frangipane

Melt the butter/margarine and set aside.

Beat the eggs well with a hand-held whisk, then add in the sugar and whisk to combine.

In another bowl, mix the tapioca flour and ground almonds until combined.

Stir the almond mix into the egg mix and beat to combine, then add the melted butter/margarine and beat well by hand.

Pour the almond mixture over the pastry and gooseberries and sprinkle with flaked almonds.

Bake in the preheated oven for 15 minutes until golden brown and the frangipane is firm.

Insert a skewer into the centre to ensure the tarts are fully baked. The skewer should come out dry.

Dust with icing sugar to serve.

Chocolate & almond torte

This is a very grown-up torte. Do try to use Marsala if you can. However, if you do not have Marsala to hand, a sweet sherry can be used instead.

100g (4oz) dark chocolate, chopped

100g (4oz) butter/margarine at room temperature, diced

1 tablespoon instant coffee powder

1 tablespoon hot water

75g (3oz) ground almonds

100g (4oz) caster sugar

3 large eggs, separated

2 tablespoons Marsala

Icing sugar, sieved, to dust

Strawberry coulis

225g (9oz) strawberries

40g (1½oz) icing sugar, sieved

Preheat the oven to Gas Mark 5/190°C/375°F. Grease a shallow 20cm/8in round cake tin and line the base and sides with baking parchment.

Combine the chocolate and butter/margarine in a bowl, standing over a saucepan of warm water. Stir over a low heat until both are melted and smooth.

Mix the coffee with the hot water.

Mix the ground almonds and sugar in a separate bowl.

Combine the chocolate mixture with the ground almond mix, then beat in the egg yolks and coffee in three batches, beating well between each addition.

In another bowl, beat the egg whites with an electric mixer, then add the Marsala and continue to beat until soft peaks form. Gently fold the chocolate mixture into the egg whites by hand using a spatula, in two batches. Pour the mixture into the prepared tin.

Bake in the preheated oven for about 45 minutes and cover with foil during baking if it looks like it's getting too brown. Leave in the cake tin once removed from the oven, cover and refrigerate for several hours or overnight.

When cold, carefully turn the cake onto a cutting board and cut into slices with a hot knife.

Before serving, make the coulis by blending the hulled strawberries and icing sugar until the mixture is smooth.

Dust the cake with sieved icing sugar and serve with the strawberry coulis and whipped cream, if desired.

Blondies tray bake

Blondies are the trendy version of brownies! I find the white chocolate version lighter and it's lovely to have a seasonal fruit blended through.

Makes 12

125g (5oz) butter/margarine

300g (12oz) white chocolate, chopped

125g (5oz) Denise's Delicious flour blend (p. 28)

1 teaspoon GF baking powder

1 teaspoon guar gum

150g (6oz) caster sugar

2 large eggs

50g (2oz) ground almonds

75g (3oz) macadamia nuts, toasted and chopped coarsely

125g (5oz) fresh or frozen raspberries

1 tablespoon icing sugar, to dust

Preheat the oven to Gas Mark 5/190°C/375°F. Grease a 23cm/9in square baking tin and line the base and sides with baking parchment.

Heat a medium-sized saucepan of water and place a bowl above the pan. Put the butter/margarine and 200g/8oz of chopped white chocolate into the bowl. Stir over a low heat, without boiling, until everything is melted and the mixture is smooth. Allow it to cool slightly.

Sieve the flour, baking powder and gum together and stir in the sugar, eggs and ground almonds until fully combined. Then stir this mixture into the melted chocolate mixture. Mix well, then stir in the remaining chopped chocolate and the nuts and raspberries.

When combined, spread into the baking tin.

Bake in the preheated oven for about 40 minutes or until firm. Cool in the tray, cut into 12 squares and dust with sieved icing sugar to serve.

Traditional Bakewell tray bake

This is an easy recipe to put together. I find it handy to make pastry in large amounts and then divide it into 450g (1lb) balls and pop into the freezer in plastic bags until I need it. The pastry freezes really well and will thaw out overnight. The recipe here is for a tray bake, but alternatively, you can grease eight individual loose-bottomed tartlet tins to make individual tarts, as shown in the photo.

Makes 8

1 quantity of sweet pastry (p. 30)

Raspberry or strawberry jam

Almond topping

200g (8oz) butter/margarine

4 large eggs

175g (7oz) caster sugar

50g (2oz) tapioca flour

150g (6oz) ground almonds

50g (2oz) flaked almonds

Prepare the pastry according to the pastry recipe instructions on page 30. While it is chilling, preheat the oven to Gas Mark 4/180°C/350°F. Grease and line a 25cm x 30cm/10in x 12in baking tray with baking parchment. Roll out the pastry on a board floured with a little potato flour.

Lifting the rolled out pastry on a rolling pin, line the baking tray with it, tucking in gently and trimming any excess with a sharp knife. If using individual tartlets, cut the pastry to fit the base of the tins and to line the sides. Press well into the sides of the tins.

Spread the jam generously on the unbaked pastry.

Almond topping

Melt the butter/margarine.

Beat the eggs well with a hand-held whisk, then add the sugar and whisk to combine.

In another bowl, mix the flour and ground almonds until combined.

Stir the almond mix into the eggs and beat with a wooden spoon to combine, then add the melted butter/margarine and beat well.

Pour the almond mixture over the pastry and jam using a spatula to guide the mixture into the corners. If baking individual tartlets, divide the mixture between the eight tins.

Sprinkle with flaked almonds and bake in the centre of the pre-heated oven for 40–50 minutes until golden brown and a skewer inserted into the almond topping comes out dry. The individual tartlets will cook much more quickly, in 10–15 minutes.

Remove from the oven and allow to cool fully in the tin before cutting into squares and serving.

Moist chocolate brownies

Ah the secret ingredient! Beetroot is one of the best-kept secrets in baking. Give these a whirl, you won't be disappointed. Just remember to buy the precooked, vacuum-packed beetroots, not the jar of pickled beetroot in vinegar!

Makes 12

50g (2oz) hazelnuts

600g (1lb 7oz) cooked beetroot with natural juice drained off

125g (5oz) Denise's Delicious flour blend (p. 28)

1 teaspoon guar gum

1 teaspoon GF baking powder

100g (4oz) cocoa powder

200g (8oz) light muscovado sugar

200g (8oz) golden syrup

6 large eggs

½ teaspoon salt

Icing sugar for dusting

Preheat the oven to Gas Mark 5/190°C/375°F. Line a 25cm x 30cm/10in x 12in Swiss roll tin with baking parchment.

Rub the hazelnuts to remove any loose skins, then whizz them in a food processor until finely ground. Add the beetroot and blend until it is a purée. Pour into a medium bowl.

In another bowl, sieve the flour, gum, baking powder and cocoa powder all together three times. This will allow the cocoa to blend properly with the flour and avoids lumps.

Add the flour mixture to the beetroot mixture.

Combine the sugar, syrup, eggs and salt and beat together with an electric mixer on setting one until smooth. Stir into the beetroot and flour mixture.

Pour the mixture into the prepared tin and bake for 35 minutes until firm in the centre but still a little sticky.

Allow to cool fully before cutting into twelve squares and, if you like, dust with icing sugar.

Crunchy flapjacks

This is a scrumptious snack for between meals. Do check that your coeliac is happy to eat pure oats before serving.

Makes 12

175g (7oz) butter/margarine

100g (4oz) brown sugar

75g (3oz) golden syrup

350g (14oz) pure oats

¼ teaspoon ginger

½ teaspoon cinnamon

200g (8oz) dark or milk chocolate (whichever you prefer)

Preheat the oven to Gas Mark 2/150°C/300°F. Grease and line a 23cm x 33cm/9in x 13in Swiss roll tin with baking parchment.

Melt the butter/margarine in a saucepan with the sugar and golden syrup. Heat gently until the sugar is dissolved.

Stir in the oats and spices.

Place the mixture into the prepared Swiss roll tin and press it out evenly using the back of a spoon.

Bake in the preheated oven for approximately 30 minutes or until golden brown.

Break the chocolate into a bowl over a saucepan of water on a medium heat and melt, stirring occasionally.

While the chocolate is still hot, pour over the flapjacks.

Chill in the fridge until the chocolate has set.

Use a hot knife to cut into twelve squares without breaking the chocolate.

Millionaire's shortbread

There's something indulgent about this recipe and it's really filling so you will only manage one square at a time. This recipe keeps really well in an airtight container for a week or so but it will be absolutely demolished before the week is over.

Makes 12

1 quantity of sweet pastry (p. 30)

Caramel

1½ small cans (580g/21oz in total) of condensed milk

300g (12oz) butter/margarine, at room temperature

150ml (5floz) or 6 tablespoons golden syrup

Topping

200g (8oz) dark chocolate

Make the pastry according to the instructions. While it is chilling, preheat the oven to Gas Mark 6/200°C/400°F. Grease and line a 25cm x 30cm/10in x 12in Swiss roll tin with baking parchment.

Roll out the pastry on a board floured with a little potato flour.

Lifting the rolled out pastry on a rolling pin, line the base of the tray only, not the sides.

Bake blind for about 15 minutes until the pastry is golden brown. There is no need to use baking beans when baking gluten-free pastry.

Caramel
Place all the ingredients in a large heavy-based saucepan over a low heat.

Stir constantly until the butter/margarine melts.

Bring to the boil, stirring continuously to prevent it burning at the edges.

Boil for 5 minutes and keep stirring to ensure the mixture doesn't burn.

Set aside to cool for 10 minutes and pour over the pastry base before the caramel is too cold.

Place in the fridge and leave for 2–3 hours until the caramel is firm.

Chocolate
Put a saucepan of water on a medium heat and place a bowl over this to make a bain marie.

Break the chocolate into the bowl and melt, stirring occasionally.

While the chocolate is still hot, pour it over the caramel and allow it to spread itself out to the edges.

Chill in the fridge until the chocolate has set. Use a hot knife to cut into twelve squares without breaking the chocolate.

Coffee & walnut Victoria sponge tray bake

There's something really comforting about a chunk of coffee cake with a thick layer of coffee buttercream. This recipe is a tribute to all our customers who love our coffee cake and feel like making some at home for the family.

Makes 12

200g (8oz) butter/margarine

125g (5oz) caster sugar

5 medium eggs

165g (6½oz) Denise's Delicious flour blend (p. 28)

3 teaspoons GF baking powder

1 teaspoon instant coffee

3 tablespoons hot water

100g (4oz) walnuts, chopped

Coffee buttercream frosting

225g (9oz) butter/margarine at room temperature

¼ teaspoon salt

60ml (2floz) milk

1 teaspoon instant coffee granules

1 teaspoon cocoa powder

580g (1lb 5oz) icing sugar, sieved

Walnuts, to decorate

Preheat the oven to Gas Mark 5/190°C/375°F. Grease and line the bottom of a deep metal baking tin measuring 25cm x 18cm/10in x 7in with baking parchment.

Cream the butter/margarine and sugar in a medium-sized bowl with an electric mixer.

Add the eggs, mixing well between each one until fully combined.

Sieve the flour and baking powder into a separate bowl.

Add it to the butter mixture, two or three tablespoons at a time, mixing well between each addition.

Blend the coffee and the hot water, mixing well, and add this to the mixture. Beat on a low speed and add the chopped walnuts and mix thoroughly. Using a spatula, put the mixture into the prepared tin and bake until golden brown and a skewer comes out dry.

Leave to cool in the tin while you make the icing.

Coffee buttercream frosting

Place the butter/margarine and salt in a large mixing bowl and beat on high with an electric mixer until light and fluffy.

Place the milk, coffee granules and cocoa in a small bowl and whisk until dissolved.

With the mixer on low, gradually add the icing sugar to the butter until combined, then increase the speed and gradually add the coffee mixture.

Beat on high until everything is fluffy and well-combined. You may need to add more sieved icing sugar if your icing is too runny. It should be smooth and fluffy, easy to spread but stiff enough to hold its shape.

Cover the sponge generously in coffee buttercream and sprinkle with walnuts. Cut into twelve squares and serve.

Chapter 7

Desserts

Cranberry bread & butter pudding

This recipe is a twist on a classic favourite of mine. If you like the centre to be very soft, then place a dish of boiling water on the floor of the oven whilst the pudding bakes.

300ml (10floz) milk

300ml (10floz) cream

6 slices gluten-free white bread (approx.), buttered

50g (2oz) dried cranberries soaked in rum and drained

3 large eggs

100g (4oz) caster sugar

Preheat the oven to Gas Mark 4/180°C/350°F. Grease an 18cm/7in round deep pie dish.

Add the milk and cream to a saucepan, gently bring to the boil and set aside.

Cut the buttered bread into fingers and arrange a layer of these in the base of the greased pie dish.

Sprinkle some of the rum-soaked cranberries on the top of the bread. Place another layer of bread, then cranberries, until all the bread is used, finishing with a layer of bread.

Mix the eggs and sugar well, then add the warm milk/cream mixture and whisk thoroughly.

Pour the liquid on top of the bread and cranberries. Allow it to settle for 5 minutes before placing in the centre of the oven.

Bake in the preheated oven for 30 minutes until golden brown.

Serve warm with some freshly whipped cream.

Delicious citrus pudding

The citrus fruits here give a summery feel to this recipe. It's a great way to add some sunshine to a winter lunch!

75g (3oz) softened butter/margarine

150g (6oz) caster sugar

3 large eggs, separated

50g (2oz) potato flour

25g (1oz) corn flour

½ teaspoon xanthan gum

1 teaspoon GF baking powder

Grated zest and juice of 1 orange

Grated zest and juice of 1 lemon

Grated zest and juice of 2 limes

210ml (7floz) milk

Icing sugar to dust

Preheat the oven to Gas Mark 5/190°C/375°F. Grease a 20cm/8in pie dish.

In a large bowl, whisk the butter/margarine and sugar together with an electric mixer until pale in colour.

Beat the egg yolks and whisk them into the mixture a little at a time.

Sieve the flours, gum and baking powder together and gently fold into the butter mixture, alternating with the combined citrus juices and zests and lastly the milk.

In a clean bowl, whisk the egg whites to the soft peak stage.

Fold the egg whites into the rest of the mixture very gently.

Pour the mixture into the prepared dish and bake it on the middle shelf of the oven for 50 minutes, by which time the top should be a nice golden brown colour.

Dust with icing sugar and serve warm with vanilla ice cream.

Sticky toffee pudding

Sticky toffee pudding is comfort food, have no doubt about it! If we're out to dinner and it's on the menu, I make sure my husband Derek orders it for himself, but with two spoons of course …

Makes 10

300g (12oz) stoned dates, chopped

240ml (8floz) boiling water

1 teaspoon vanilla extract

2 teaspoons coffee essence

1½ teaspoons bread soda, sieved

150g (6oz) butter/margarine

250g (10oz) caster sugar

4 large eggs, beaten

300g (12oz) Denise's Delicious flour blend (p. 28)

½ teaspoon GF baking powder

½ teaspoon xanthan gum

Extra margarine and potato flour for greasing dariole moulds

Sauce

75g (3oz) butter/margarine

50g (2oz) brown sugar

2 tablespoons cream

50g (2oz) pecan nuts, chopped

Preheat the oven to Gas Mark 4/180°C/350°F. Grease and flour ten 7½cm/3in diameter dariole moulds, shaking out any excess flour.

Place the chopped dates in the boiling water. Add the vanilla extract, coffee essence and bread soda, stir and set aside.

Cream the butter/margarine and sugar with an electric beater until fluffy.

Beat in the eggs one at a time.

Sieve the flour, baking powder and gum and fold into the butter mixture. Then fold the date mixture into the cake mixture.

Half fill the moulds with the pudding mixture. Place on a baking tray and bake for 25 minutes. When cooked they will have risen and be spongy to the touch and an inserted skewer will come out dry.

Sauce

Just before serving, prepare the sauce. Melt the butter/margarine over a gentle heat, and stir in the sugar until dissolved.

Stir in the cream, mix well and add the pecan nuts.

To serve, turn out the puddings onto serving plates and spoon the sauce over them. Serve warm.

Rhubarb & apple queen of puddings

Another recipe from Mum's repertoire. Traditionally it is baked with raspberry jam but I like to add fruit to mine. This is a great recipe for using up stale bread.

4 sticks fresh rhubarb

3 eating apples

60ml (2floz) water

Caster sugar to sweeten the fruit

600ml (20floz) milk

15g (½oz) butter/margarine

50g (2oz) caster sugar, plus 1 teaspoon

100g (4oz) fresh gluten-free breadcrumbs

Grated zest of 1 lemon

2 large eggs

Preheat the oven to Gas Mark 4/180°C/350°F. Generously grease an 850ml/1½ pint deep oval pie dish with butter/margarine.

Top and tail the rhubarb and cut into cubes. Peel and core the apples and cut in cubes or slices.

Simmer the rhubarb and apple in a medium-sized saucepan with the water over a low heat, until the fruit is soft but still holds its shape.

Add caster sugar to taste: this will depend on how tart the rhubarb is. Set aside to cool.

Pour the milk into a saucepan and bring to the boil.

Remove from the heat and add in the butter/margarine and 25g (1oz) of the sugar and stir. Then add the breadcrumbs and the lemon zest and leave for 20 minutes to allow the breadcrumbs to swell.

Separate the eggs, beat the yolks and add them to the cooled breadcrumb mixture.

Pour the mixture into the pie dish and spread it out evenly. Allow it to sit for 5 minutes before baking.

Bake in the centre of the oven for 30–35 minutes until set.

Remove from the oven and spoon the poached fruit on top of the breadcrumb mixture.

Beat the egg whites until stiff, then whisk in 25g (1oz) of caster sugar until glossy and spoon this meringue mixture over the pudding.

Finally, sprinkle a teaspoon of caster sugar over it all and bake for a further 10–15 minutes until the topping is golden brown.

Vanilla soufflé

Julia Childs is the most wonderful of chefs and her books are a must. My mum bought us a hostess trolley for dinner parties (to keep the food hot) and we have christened it Julia in honour of Julia Childs. It is from her books that I learned to make a good soufflé, so this is my tribute to the lovely Julia.

20g (¾oz) potato flour

½ teaspoon guar gum

150ml (5floz) milk

50g (2oz) caster sugar, plus 1 tablespoon and extra for dusting

4 large eggs, separated, plus 1 extra egg white

25g (1oz) butter/margarine, softened

Pinch of salt

3 teaspoons vanilla extract

Icing sugar to sprinkle

To serve

Strawberries

Balsamic vinegar

Vanilla ice cream

Preheat the oven to Gas Mark 5/190°C/375°F. Grease a 14cm/5½in diameter, 9cm/3½in deep soufflé dish very well and shake some sugar around in it to coat the sides and bottom evenly. Knock out the excess sugar and set the dish aside.

Mix the flour and gum. In a saucepan, beat the flour with a little of the milk until blended. Add the rest of the milk and 50g (2oz) of the caster sugar and beat to combine.

Stir the mixture over a moderate heat until it has thickened and comes to the boil. Boil, whilst stirring, for 30 seconds, remove from the heat and beat for 2 minutes to allow it to cool slightly.

Add the egg yolks one at a time, beating well between each addition.

Beat in half of the butter/margarine and use a spatula to make sure all is well mixed. Dab the remaining butter/margarine on top of the mixture to stop a skin forming.

Beat the five egg whites and the salt until soft peaks form. Sprinkle on the tablespoon of sugar and continue to beat until stiff peaks are formed.

Beat the vanilla extract into the cooled mixture. Then gently fold in the egg whites in four batches.

Fill the soufflé dish and leave approximately 4cm/1½in at the top for the soufflé to rise. If the mould is too full, the soufflé will spill out as it bakes.

Place the soufflé in the middle of the oven.

After 25 minutes, when it has started to puff and brown, quickly but gently open the oven door and sprinkle the soufflé with icing sugar. Close the oven door gently and continue to bake for a further 5–10 minutes.

To check it is cooked, gently insert a skewer through the side of the soufflé, which should come out clean.

Serve immediately with the strawberries tossed in balsamic vinegar on the side and some vanilla ice cream.

New York-style baked cheesecake

I much prefer a baked cheesecake to a chilled cheesecake. The texture of a baked cheesecake is very different and I find it to be creamier. Follow the baking instructions carefully to ensure the cheesecake does not crack.

125g (5oz) Denise's Delicious flour blend (p. 28)

½ teaspoon xanthan gum

75g (3oz) butter/margarine

200g (8oz) caster sugar

1 small whole egg and 2 small eggs, separated

325g (13oz) cream cheese

250g (10oz) sour cream

25g (1oz) corn flour

Zest and juice of half an orange

Zest and juice of half a lemon

¼ teaspoon vanilla extract

Caramelised lemon

2 lemons, sliced thinly

115g (4½oz) caster sugar

150ml (5floz) water

Preheat the oven to Gas Mark 6/200°C/400°F. Grease an 18cm/7in round spring base tin.

Sieve the flour and gum, then rub in the butter/margarine.

Add 50g (2oz) of the caster sugar and stir in.

Beat the whole egg lightly and mix into the dry ingredients to form a paste. Refrigerate for half an hour before rolling out.

When chilled, roll the pastry out on a floured board and line the bottom of the baking tin.

Beat 150g (6oz) of the caster sugar and the cream cheese together until smooth. Then add the sour cream and mix again. Mix the egg yolks and corn flour in a separate bowl, then mix in.

In a separate clean bowl, beat the egg whites until they form peaks and fold them into the mixture. Finally, fold in the zests, juices and vanilla extract. Mix all to a smooth consistency.

Pour onto the prepared base and bake at Gas Mark 6/200°C/400°F for the first 10 minutes, then adjust the oven to Gas Mark 4/180°C/350°F for a further 50 minutes, until the centre is set.

Caramelised lemon

While the cheesecake is cooking, put the lemon slices (discarding any seeds), sugar and water in a small heavy-based saucepan and bring to the boil, then simmer for about 45 minutes, shaking the pan occasionally, until most of the liquid has evaporated and the lemons have caramelised.

Watch very carefully towards the end of cooking that the lemons don't burn. Drain the lemon slices on a wire rack.

When the cheesecake has cooled completely, carefully remove from the tin and decorate with the caramelised lemons.

Plum crème brûlée

I love to eat crème brûleé wherever I go and every baker has their own way of making this. I like mine to be served at room temperature, but the norm is to have it chilled. It is essential that the crème brûlée does not boil or you will have a sorry scrambled mess on your hands. To be safe, I prefer to thicken it over a bain marie.

6 plums

175g (7oz) caster sugar

450ml (15floz) cream

½ vanilla pod

5 large egg yolks

Pinch of potato flour

Brown sugar for brûlée topping

Grease 6–8 ramekin dishes well.

Bring a pot of water to the boil, then remove it from the heat. Score the skin of the plums and pop gently into the boiled water. This will cause the skins to shrivel. Allow them to rest in the water for 2–3 minutes. Carefully remove and peel the skins from them with a sharp knife. Be careful as the plums are hot! Allow the plums to cool, then cut them in half to remove the stones and chop them into rough cubes.

Place the fruit in a pan and add cold water to half the depth of the fruit.

Simmer, covered, over a low heat and allow the fruit to poach.

When softened, but still holding their shape, add 100g (4oz) of caster sugar one dessertspoon at a time.

In a separate saucepan, heat the cream and vanilla pod and bring to the boil. Remove the vanilla pod, split it and scrape the insides of the pod into the cream and stir in.

Whisk 75g (3oz) of caster sugar and the egg yolks together. Add the potato flour while whisking.

Remove the cooled plums from the syrup with a slotted spoon and put them in the bottom of the ramekin dishes – enough to cover the base.

Whisk the vanilla cream into the egg and sugar mixture.

Return to the saucepan, or to a bain marie, and heat gently while stirring continuously to avoid scrambling. It is essential this does not come to the boil.

When thickened, pour this over the fruit. Chill in the fridge overnight.

Before serving, sprinkle each ramekin with sugar and, with a cook's blowtorch, caramelise the sugar on top. If you do not have a blowtorch, place the brûlée under a very hot grill until the sugar melts.

Fresh cherry clafoutis

This is a classic French recipe and is wonderful when fresh cherries are in season. Do be careful of your hands as cherries will stain badly. It is not a look that you need with your newly applied manicure! This recipe works well with rhubarb or poached apple when cherries are out of season.

3 large eggs

125g (5oz) caster sugar

50g (2oz) corn flour

50g (2oz) rice flour

½ teaspoon of GF baking powder

210ml (7floz) crème fraîche

450g (1lb) cherries

Butter/margarine and sugar to line dish

Icing sugar to dust

Preheat the oven to Gas Mark 5/190°C/375°F. Grease a 20cm/8in pie dish and sprinkle with sugar.

Lightly whisk the eggs with the sugar by hand for approximately 1 minute until mousse-like.

Sieve the flours and baking powder together. Add this to the egg mixture and whisk, then stir in the crème fraîche.

Prepare the cherries by washing, removing stalks and coring them to remove the stones.

Put the fruit in the prepared dish and pour over the batter.

Cook in the preheated oven for 45 minutes, until golden brown and a skewer comes out dry.

Dust with icing sugar and serve.

Crêpe Suzette

Crêpe Suzette is one of those wonderful retro desserts. Make sure to flambé them at the end. It adds a little theatre to the evening!

Makes 8–10

Crêpe batter

50g (2oz) potato flour

25g (1oz) tapioca flour

25g (1oz) corn flour

¼ teaspoon xanthan gum

Pinch of salt

2 large eggs

210ml (7floz) milk mixed with 90ml (3floz) water

2 tablespoons melted butter/margarine

A little extra butter/margarine for cooking the pancakes

For the sauce

Juice of 3–4 oranges (150ml/5floz)

Grated zest of 1 medium orange

Grated zest and juice of 1 small lemon

1 tablespoon caster sugar

3 tablespoons Grand Marnier or brandy

50g (2oz) butter/margarine

For the flambé

80–100ml (2½–3½floz) Grand Marnier

Sieve the flours, gum and salt into a large mixing bowl.

Make a well in the centre and break the eggs into it.

Start to whisk the eggs, beginning to incorporate flour from around the edges as you do so.

Gradually start to add the milk and water.

When all the milk and water has been added, run a rubber spatula around the edge of the bowl to make sure all the mixture is incorporated.

Whisk once more until the batter is smooth and the consistency of thin cream.

Before cooking, add the two tablespoons of melted butter/margarine to the batter and stir it in. Then melt about a teaspoon of butter/margarine in the pan and swirl it all around to cover the base of the pan completely.

Once the pan is really hot turn the heat down to medium. Use approximately 1¾ tablespoons of batter for each crêpe.

Pour the batter into the frying pan and rotate the pan until the batter forms a nice circular shape. Allow the batter to set and then use a fish slice to turn the crêpe.

Cook until golden brown on both sides. Repeat until all the batter is used. This should make 8–10 crêpes.

For the sauce

When you have cooked and stacked the crêpes, use a small bowl to mix together all the sauce ingredients, except the butter/margarine.

Warm the plates on which the crêpes are to be served.

Take a large frying pan and melt the butter/ margarine in it. Add the other sauce ingredients and allow it to heat very gently.

Place the first crêpe in the pan, give it time to warm through, then fold it in half and half again, to make a triangle shape. Slide it to the very edge of the pan.

Tilt the pan slightly so that the sauce runs back into the centre, then add the next crêpe and continue until they are all reheated, folded and soaked with the sauce.

Place all on a serving plate.

For the flambé

Warm the extra Grand Marnier in the emptied frying pan. Using a long handled gas lighter, set the liqueur alight.

Carry the pancakes to the table and pour the flambé over them to serve.

Chocolate mousse with roast pineapple

This is a wonderful luscious after-dinner treat. Serve small portions as this is really rich. The roast pineapple provides a wonderfully refreshing foil for the mousse.

Makes 4 servings

75g (3oz) dark chocolate, finely chopped

2 tablespoons water, brandy or rum

15g (½oz) butter/margarine, at room temperature

3 large eggs, separated

To serve

1 pineapple

3 teaspoons cinnamon

Put the chocolate and water, brandy or rum into a heatproof bowl set over a saucepan of steaming but not boiling water and leave until just melted. Make sure not to let the base of the bowl touch the water.

Remove the bowl from the heat and gently stir in the butter/margarine.

Leave for 1 minute, then gently whisk in the egg yolks, one at a time.

Put the egg whites into a clean, grease-free bowl and whisk with an electric whisk or mixer until stiff peaks form.

Gently stir about one-quarter of the egg whites into the chocolate mixture to loosen it, then using a large metal spoon, gently fold in the rest of the egg whites in three batches.

Carefully spoon into four serving bowls, cups or glasses, then chill for 2 hours before serving.

To serve

30 minutes before serving, preheat the oven to Gas Mark 3/165°C/325°F.

Peel core and slice the pineapple and sprinkle generously with cinnamon.

Place on a baking tray and roast in the oven for 20 minutes.

Cut into chunks and serve alongside the chilled chocolate mousse.

Almond & raspberry meringue cake

This is an unusual combination of chewy meringue, almonds and moist chocolate cake. The raspberries marry well with the almonds; this is also lovely with poached clementines.

115g (4½oz) butter/margarine, chopped

250g (10oz) caster sugar

3 large eggs, separated

120ml (4floz) buttermilk

135ml (4½floz) sour cream

125g (5oz) Denise's Delicious flour blend (p. 28)

1 teaspoon GF baking powder

½ teaspoon xanthan gum

25g (1oz) cocoa powder

2 tablespoons flaked almonds

To decorate

180ml (6floz) whipping cream

1 tablespoon icing sugar

125g (5oz) fresh raspberries

Preheat the oven to Gas Mark 5/190°C/375°F. Grease two deep 23cm/9in round cake tins and line the bases with baking parchment.

Beat the butter/margarine, 100g (4oz) of sugar and the egg yolks in a medium bowl with an electric mixer until light and fluffy.

Separately, combine the buttermilk and sour cream and whisk until blended.

Sieve the flour, baking powder, gum and cocoa powder three times to remove lumps and to ensure the cocoa blends properly. Stir the dry ingredients into the butter mixture, then mix in the combined buttermilk and sour cream. Divide the mixture evenly between the prepared tins.

Beat the egg whites in a small bowl with an electric mixer until soft peaks form. Gradually add 150g (6oz) of sugar, one tablespoon at a time, beating until the sugar dissolves between additions and the egg whites become glossy.

Divide the meringue mixture evenly between the tins, spreading the meringue so that the cake mixture is completely covered. Sprinkle flaked almonds over the meringue on one of the cakes.

Bake the cakes in the oven for 10 minutes, then cover the tins loosely with foil and bake for about another 20 minutes. Discard the foil and gently skewer to check if fully baked.

Stand the cakes in their tins for 5 minutes, before turning onto wire racks. Quickly and carefully turn the cakes top-side up to cool.

Beat the cream and icing sugar in a small bowl with an electric mixer until firm peaks form. Place the cake without almonds on a serving plate; spread cream over the top, sprinkle evenly with raspberries and top with the remaining cake with the flaked almonds on top.

Orange-infused chocolate truffles

Truffles are indulgent and a wonderful way to round off a dinner party. These are handmade, so don't worry if they aren't perfectly shaped!

Makes 14–16

For the truffles

210ml (7floz) double cream

300g (12oz) dark chocolate, finely chopped

To coat

225g (9oz) dark or white chocolate, chopped

3–4 drops natural orange essence

50g (2oz) finest quality cocoa powder

Line two baking trays with baking parchment.

Put the cream into a saucepan and heat gently until boiling. Remove from the heat and allow to cool for several minutes.

Put the chopped chocolate into a heatproof bowl, then pour the cream over the chocolate. Set aside for a couple of minutes.

Stir gently until just smooth. Do not over-mix at this stage. Allow to cool in the fridge for 10–15 minutes.

When the mixture is cold but not set, beat vigorously with a wooden spoon, or on speed one of an electric mixer, until very thick and much lighter in colour and texture.

The mixture will be quite stiff now. Roll some of the mixture in your hands to form a round, marble-sized ball, then place it on a baking tray. Repeat until all the mixture is used. Place in the fridge for several hours.

When ready to finish the truffles, put the chopped chocolate and orange essence into a heatproof bowl and set over a saucepan of steaming but not boiling water. The water should not touch the base of the bowl or start to boil. When the chocolate is melted remove the bowl from the heat.

Using two forks, briefly dip each truffle into the chocolate until fully coated.

Return the coated truffles to the baking trays and leave until the coating chocolate is almost set.

While the coating chocolate is still slightly soft, roll the truffles in cocoa powder. Store in the fridge until ready to serve.

Raspberry vacherin

I never quite understood the link between vacherin cheese and a dessert, as raspberry vacherin has nothing to do with cheese. Nevertheless, this is another easy recipe that looks great and will impress the in-laws at a dinner party!

3 large egg whites

150g (6oz) caster sugar

1 teaspoon corn flour

25g (1oz) dark chocolate, grated

Filling and topping

150g (6oz) dark chocolate, broken into pieces

450ml (15floz) double cream, whipped

250g (10oz) fresh raspberries

A little melted chocolate to decorate

Preheat the oven to Gas Mark 1/140°C/275°F. Draw three rectangles, measuring 10cm x 25cm/4in x 10in on baking parchment. Cut these out and place on two baking trays.

Whisk the egg whites in a mixing bowl until soft peaks form, then gradually whisk in half the sugar and continue whisking until the mixture is very stiff and glossy.

Fold in the remaining sugar, the corn flour and the grated chocolate. Spoon the meringue mixture into a piping bag fitted with a 1cm/½in plain nozzle and pipe lines across the rectangles. You want to have three rectangular pieces of meringue that are the same size.

Bake in the preheated oven for 1½ hours. Then turn off the oven and leave the meringues to cool inside the oven. When cold, peel away the baking parchment.

To assemble

When the meringue is completely cold, place the broken chocolate into a heatproof bowl set over a saucepan of gently simmering water until melted. Spread the chocolate over two of the meringue layers. Leave to harden.

Place one chocolate-coated meringue on a plate and top with one third of the cream and raspberries. Gently place the second chocolate-coated meringue on top and spread with half of the remaining cream and raspberries. Place the last meringue on the top and spread with the remaining cream and raspberries. Drizzle the melted chocolate over the top of the vacherin and serve.

Passion fruit meringue kisses

These are very cute and are lovely to serve with afternoon tea. Show these off on a pretty glass cake stand.

Makes 6–8

1 large egg white

½ teaspoon white vinegar

75g (3oz) caster sugar

1 teaspoon icing sugar

60ml (2floz) whipping cream

1 tablespoon icing sugar

1 tablespoon passion fruit pulp

Extra icing sugar, to dust

Preheat the oven to Gas Mark ½/130°C/250°F. Grease two 36cm x 26cm/14in x 10in baking trays and cover with a piece of parchment paper.

Beat the egg white, vinegar and caster sugar in a small bowl with an electric mixer for about 10 minutes or until the caster sugar dissolves. Then fold in the icing sugar.

Place the meringue mixture in a piping bag fitted with a small plain nozzle and pipe 1½cm/½in rounds, 3cm/1¼in apart, on the prepared trays.

Bake in the preheated oven for about 30 minutes or until crisp and dry. Remove from the oven and allow them to cool on the baking trays.

Beat the cream, one tablespoon of icing sugar and the passion fruit pulp in a small bowl with an electric mixer until stiff peaks form.

Sandwich two meringues together with passion fruit cream, then dust with the extra icing sugar.

Vanilla pavlova with mixed fruits

Pavlova is one of those easy recipes that everyone thinks is very complex. Pavlova scares a lot of people but follow these fail-safe steps for a sure thing.

6 large egg whites

275g (11oz) caster sugar

½ teaspoon vanilla extract

1 teaspoon corn flour

½ teaspoon white vinegar

480ml (16floz) cream

200g (8oz) mixed fruits

Chocolate curls and icing sugar to decorate

Preheat the oven to Gas Mark 2/150°C/300°F. Grease a flat 36cm x 26cm/14in x 10in baking tray lightly and cover with baking parchment.

Place the egg whites in a clean, dry mixing bowl with no trace of oil or grease.

Mix with an electric mixer on setting two for 2–3 minutes until the egg whites become firm and hold their shape.

Add the sugar one dessertspoon at a time until the egg whites become glossy and velvety. The test is to turn the bowl upside down – when the mix is ready it is so stiff that it doesn't move.

Add the vanilla extract, corn flour and vinegar and mix gently for 30 seconds on setting one.

Using a spatula, spoon the mixture onto the baking tray forming a rectangular shape.

Place in the preheated oven for about 70–80 minutes. Keep the oven door closed. As it bakes the colour will change from gleaming white to pale beige.

Turn off the oven but leave the pavlova in the oven to cool. When ready to dress it, gently slip it off the baking parchment onto a presentation dish.

To dress with a casual look, whip the cream loosely and pile onto the pavlova, spreading to the edge. Pile the fruit into the centre.

If you like, you can sprinkle chocolate curls all over the pavlova and dust with sieved icing sugar to finish.

Chocolate roulade

Chocolate roulades always crack when rolled, so do not fret. Dust with lots of icing sugar. This is a wonderful centrepiece dessert.

6 large egg whites

40g (1½oz) cocoa powder

275g (11oz) caster sugar

50g (2oz) icing sugar, for dusting

Chocolate mousse filling

200g (8oz) dark chocolate

2 tablespoons water

2 large eggs, separated

To assemble

240ml (8floz) double cream

Fresh raspberries and icing sugar to decorate

Preheat the oven to Gas Mark 2/150°C/300°F. Grease a flat 36cm x 26cm/14in x 10in baking tray lightly and cover with baking parchment.

Place the egg whites in a clean, dry mixing bowl with no trace of oil or grease.

Mix with an electric mixer on setting two for 2–3 minutes until soft peaks are formed.

Sieve the cocoa into the caster sugar and mix well.

Add the cocoa–sugar mixture to the egg whites, with the mixer running, one dessertspoon at a time until the egg whites become glossy and velvety. The test is to turn the bowl upside down – when the mix is ready it is so stiff that it doesn't move.

Using a spatula, spoon the mixture onto the baking tray forming a rectangular shape.

Place in the preheated oven for about 70–80 minutes. Keep the oven door closed.

Take a piece of baking parchment, place on a flat surface and sieve icing sugar all over it.

When it is cooked, remove the roulade from the oven and gently turn it out on the baking parchment and cover with a damp tea towel.

Chocolate mousse filling

Break the chocolate into pieces and place it, along with the water, in a bowl. Place the bowl over a saucepan of water on a medium heat, stirring until the chocolate is smooth.

Take off the heat and set aside to cool.

Gently beat the egg yolks into the chocolate and whisk well.

Whisk the egg whites in a clean bowl with an electric mixer until soft peaks form.

Fold the egg whites gently into the chocolate mixture until fully incorporated.

To assemble

Whip the cream and spread gently over the roulade.

Next, gently spread the chocolate mousse over the roulade. Then, starting at the short end of the roulade, roll the roulade slowly, using the baking parchment to keep it together.

Remove the baking parchment and gently move the roulade to a serving plate, being careful how you lift the roulade. A large fish slice is very useful to prevent the roulade from breaking.

Store in the fridge until ready to serve, then dust liberally with sieved icing sugar and dress with raspberries.

Chapter 8

Christmas

Jack Frost muffins

I love to have these muffins on Christmas Eve morning – I feel Christmas has arrived properly then. I mix all the dry ingredients the night before and have my other ingredients ready in the fridge. It just takes three minutes in the morning to put it all together. Make sure to play some Christmas music for yourself while you enjoy these treats!

Makes 12

200g (8oz) Denise's Delicious flour blend (p. 28)

½ teaspoon GF baking powder

½ teaspoon bread soda

1 teaspoon mixed spice

75g (3oz) demerara sugar

90ml (3floz) orange juice

60ml (2floz) milk

1 medium egg

50g (2oz) butter/margarine, melted

125g (5oz) dried cranberries

For the topping

2 teaspoons demerara sugar

½ teaspoon mixed spice

Preheat the oven to Gas Mark 5/190°C/375°F. Line a twelve-hole muffin tin with paper cases.

In a large bowl, sieve the flour, baking powder, bread soda and spice together. Add the sugar and mix together.

In another bowl, pour in the orange juice, add the milk and egg, and beat until combined. Don't worry if it curdles a bit. Add the melted margarine and beat again.

Remembering that a lumpy batter makes light muffins, start mixing very lightly by hand, adding the wet ingredients to the dry. Do not beat or the muffins will be leathery and small. Gently add the cranberries and stir in lightly.

Spoon into the muffin cases.

For the topping, mix the sugar and mixed spice and sprinkle on top before placing in the centre of the oven.

Bake for 15–20 minutes until golden brown and a skewer inserted into the centre comes out dry.

Remove from the oven and remove from the baking tin after 2–3 minutes. Allow to cool on a wire rack. When completely cool, store in an airtight container.

Before serving dust with icing sugar.

Christmas cake

This is a lovely recipe and making your own Christmas cake is very symbolic. Make sure that everyone in the house gives the mixture a stir for good luck!

450g (1lb) golden sultanas

200g (8oz) raisins

150g (6oz) currants

3 tablespoons brandy

200g (8oz) Denise's Delicious flour blend (p. 28)

1 teaspoon xanthan gum

½ teaspoon salt

1 teaspoon mixed spice

175g (7oz) butter/margarine

200g (8oz) demerara sugar

4 large eggs, lightly beaten

50g (2oz) nibbed almonds

100g (4oz) natural glacé cherries, washed, chopped and rolled in ground almonds

Grated zest and juice of 1 orange

Grated zest of 1 lemon

2–3 tablespoons brandy to pour over the cooked cake

To decorate

Marzipan (p. 198)

Royal icing (p. 200)

Place the sultanas, raisins and currants in a bowl. Add the brandy and mix. Cover and allow them to stand overnight.

Heat the oven to Gas Mark 2/150°C/300°F. The temperature is very low as the cake needs a long, slow bake.

Line a 23cm/9in cake tin with three layers of baking parchment or greaseproof paper.

Sieve the flour, gum, salt and spice into a bowl and set aside.

In another large bowl, cream the butter/margarine with the sugar until light and fluffy.

Add the beaten eggs to the butter mixture a little bit at a time, beating well after each addition – do not try to rush this process.

Carefully fold half the flour mixture and half the soaked fruit into the butter mixture. Once incorporated, repeat with the remaining flour, fruit, nibbed almonds and finally the cherries.

Stir in the orange and lemon zest and orange juice.

Spoon the cake mixture into the prepared cake tin.

Once filled, smooth the surface of the cake with the back of a spoon and make a slight dip in the centre (this will rise back up again during cooking and create a smooth surface for icing the cake).

Finally, using a piece of paper towel, clean up any smears of cake batter on the baking parchment – if left on they will burn.

Stand in the centre of the oven and bake for approximately 4½ hours. If the cake is browning too rapidly, cover the tin with a double layer of greaseproof or baking parchment after 2½ hours. During the cooking time, avoid opening the oven door too often as this may cause the cake to collapse.

After 4½ hours, check the cake is baked. The cake should be nicely risen and a deep brown all over. Insert a skewer or fine knife into the centre of the cake. If there is sticky dough on the skewer when you pull it out, then it needs a little more time; if it is clean, the cake is baked.

Leave the cake to cool in the tin on a wire rack for an hour, then remove from the tin and leave to cool completely.

Once completely cool prick the surface of the cake with a fine metal skewer and slowly pour over 2–3 tablespoons of brandy.

The cake should be stored wrapped in greaseproof paper or baking parchment and a layer of tinfoil in an airtight tin.

To decorate, see the marzipan and royal icing recipes that follow.

Homemade marzipan

I find this easier to do in an electric mixer/food processor rather than by hand. Ideally this should be applied to the cake a week before the royal icing.

200g (8oz) caster sugar

200g (8oz) icing sugar

450g (1lb) ground almonds

2 large egg yolks, beaten

Apricot jam

Sieve the sugars together and mix well.

Stir in the almonds until fully blended.

Add in the beaten egg yolk gradually and mix until a firm paste – you many not need to use it all. This should be the consistency of a stiff pastry and not sticky.

Wrap in cling film and chill in the fridge until ready to use.

To decorate the Christmas cake

Roll out the marzipan on a board sprinkled with a little icing sugar. Make sure to cover the rolling pin as well.

This can be sticky to work with, so it may work better for you to roll the marzipan out between two layers of cling film.

Try to roll out the marzipan in a round shape and ensure that it is big enough to cover the top and sides of your cake.

You may be able to measure this by looking at the cake, but you may find it easier to use a piece of string or a ruler to measure the sides of the cake and the top and then use the string to measure the rolled out marzipan. This ensures that the marzipan will cover the top and sides of the cake. You can patch it if it isn't exactly right, but the more accurate you are, the easier it is.

Turn the Christmas cake upside down onto a cake board. You will be icing the base of the cake to ensure you have a flat, even surface.

Whilst upside down on the cake board, the cake should be quite flat and it should not be wobbly when you stand it on its head. If it is a little wobbly, tuck in small balls of marzipan to secure the cake on the board.

Brush the top of the cake with some warmed apricot jam and brush the sides also.

If using cling film to help with the rolling, peel back the top layer gently. Then, using the edges of the cling film, pick it up and gently invert it over the cake so that the marzipan is facing the cake and the cling film is facing upwards.

Use the cling film to allow you to mould the marzipan over the top of the cake and down the sides.

If not using cling film, then roll the marzipan around the rolling pin to move it. Line up your marzipan over the cake and when you feel you have it correctly aligned, unroll the marzipan gently from the rolling pin.

Dust your hands with a little icing sugar and pat the marzipan into place, smoothing out any bumps and making it as even as possible.

If any holes have appeared, then take a little marzipan from the bottom, where you will have a little spare, and gently pat it over the hole, moulding it into place with your fingertips.

Trim the ends of the marzipan neatly, so that it reaches the cake board.

If there is a gap between the base of the cake and the board, then roll a long sausage of marzipan between your hands and fill the gap all around the cake, so there is no gap between the cake and the cake board.

Leave the cake aside, ideally for a week, for it to dry out. Keep it covered with a clean tea towel.

Royal icing for Christmas cake

This may be a step too far for you and you may prefer to buy a pre-made roll-out icing, and a pre-made marzipan for that matter! If that is the case, ensure that it is gluten-free. For those of you who want to go the full nine yards and use a royal icing, here is the final step.

3 large egg whites

500g (1lb 2oz) icing sugar, sieved

1 teaspoon glycerine

Place the egg whites in a bowl and, with an electric whisk, mix in the sugar two tablespoons at a time until it forms stiff peaks.

Stir in the glycerine and whisk to ensure it is fully blended.

Place the cake on a turntable.

Spread the royal icing on top of the cake using a palette knife.

Make sure to work over any air bubbles to smooth them out.

Continue smoothing the icing down the sides of the cake over the marzipan.

Leave to dry for 24 hours, away from curious little ones who may be tempted to leave their fingerprints on the cake!

When dry, dress the cake with a Christmas ribbon or a collar around it and with some Christmas decorations on top.

Christmas stollen

This is a wonderful alternative to a traditional Christmas cake and is definitely one for those of you who love marzipan! This recipe makes two stollens.

50g (2oz) natural glacé cherries, chopped

50g (2oz) sultanas

50g (2oz) seedless raisins

25g (1oz) angelica, chopped

25g (1oz) mixed peel, chopped finely

6 tablespoons rum

910g (32oz) Denise's Delicious flour blend (p. 28)

1 teaspoon xanthan gum

½ teaspoon salt

8g (1 sachet) dried yeast

100g (4oz) caster sugar

1 teaspoon finely grated lemon zest

300ml (10floz) milk

2 large eggs, beaten

100g (4oz) butter/margarine, melted

50g (2oz) flaked almonds

Icing sugar for dusting

Marzipan

450g (1lb) of marzipan
(p. 198; half quantity)

Put the cherries, sultanas, raisins, angelica and mixed peel into a bowl. Add the rum, cover and leave to soak overnight.

Grease and cover a 36cm x 26cm /14in x 10in baking tray with baking parchment.

Sieve the flour, gum and salt into a large bowl and stir in the dried yeast.

Stir in the sugar and lemon zest.

Heat the milk until it is lukewarm and then add to the beaten eggs with the melted butter/margarine, stirring well.

Make a well in the centre of the flour and add the milk mixture, stirring to combine.

Gather the dough together and knead on a floured work surface until smooth – this should take about 10–15 minutes.

Drain the soaked fruit well and pat dry on a paper towel. Press the fruit and flaked almonds into the dough and knead lightly to incorporate it. Be careful at this stage not to tear the fruit or the cake will become discoloured. Keep your hands lightly floured to make it more manageable.

Place in a large greased bowl, cover with cling film and leave to rise in a warm place until doubled in size (about 2 hours).

'Knock back' the dough gently by kneading lightly until smooth. Divide into two equal parts. Roll each piece into a strip about 30cm x 20cm/12in x 8in. Then divide the marzipan into two pieces and roll into sausage shapes about 25cm/10in long.

Lay the marzipan on the dough, fold over and seal. Transfer to the greased baking tray and leave to rise again until doubled in size, covered lightly with a clean tea towel.

Preheat the oven to Gas Mark 5/190°C/375°F.

Bake the loaves in the oven for about 30–35 minutes, until golden brown.

Leave to cool on a wire rack and then dust with plenty of sieved icing sugar.

Christmas pudding

I like to reheat my pudding one slice at a time so I pop it in the microwave. Alternatively, individual mini puddings are a lovely option and they steam much more quickly. Although they are fiddly to work with, i.e. to secure the tinfoil and string, they do look very pretty when served!

75g (3oz) Denise's Delicious flour blend (p. 28)

½ teaspoon xanthan gum

100g (4oz) gluten-free breadcrumbs

1 teaspoon allspice

1 teaspoon cinnamon

150g (6oz) brown sugar

300g (12oz) raisins

100g (4oz) currants

150g (6oz) sultanas

25g (1oz) nibbed almonds

2 eating apples, cored, peeled and chopped

1 orange, zest and juice

1 lemon, zest and juice

3 large eggs

4 tablespoons rum

2 tablespoons gravy browning

Prepare two or three 450g/1lb pudding bowls or twelve mini pudding bowls. To prepare the pudding bowls, cut greaseproof paper circles by inverting the pudding bowls and drawing a circle around them. Cut around with scissors.

Put the flour, gum, breadcrumbs, spices and sugar into a bowl, one at a time, mixing in each ingredient thoroughly before adding the next. Then gradually mix in all the dried fruit and nuts and follow these with the chopped apple and orange and lemon zest.

In a different bowl, beat the eggs and mix in the rum, gravy browning (to give a nice rich colour), orange and lemon juice. Add this to the dry ingredients and then stir very hard. You may need a little more egg – it is not possible to be exact with the liquid quantities, but the mixture should be of a good dropping consistency.

After mixing, cover the bowl with a cloth and leave it overnight. The next day, mix thoroughly again. Grease the pudding basins. If you can buy pudding bowls with matching lids, it is very handy at this stage. If not, follow these steps:

1. Prepare one large pot of boiling water with a lid. The pot should be large enough to fit all the pudding basins.

2. Spoon the pudding mixture into the bowls, right up to the top.

3. Cover each bowl with a circle of greaseproof paper and tuck in. Place a larger circle of tinfoil on top, making a pleat in the centre

of it, to allow it to expand. Secure the tinfoil in place around the rims of the bowls with string. Knot the string securely to hold the tinfoil in place.

Steam the puddings gently in the saucepan for 2½ hours, watching the water to make sure it does not boil away. If you have the pudding bowls with snap on lids, it is very easy to pop them off to make sure that they are fully baked by inserting a skewer, which should come out without any uncooked mixture on it. If not fully steamed, then return to the heat.

When cooked and cooled, remove the tinfoil and greaseproof paper and replace with fresh tinfoil and greaseproof paper. Tie the tinfoil around the rims of the bowls with string; knot the string securely to hold the tinfoil in place.

Store in a cool dry place (for up to a year) and when ready to eat, steam for 2 hours to heat through (or heat individual slices in the microwave).

Mince pies with homemade mincemeat

These are the most popular pies we bake and we make hundreds of thousands. It's nice to say that you have baked them yourself; however, if it's all a bit daunting, use our pastry mix and mincemeat to make it a bit easier on yourself!

Mincemeat

200g (8oz) butter/margarine

450g (1lb) cooking apples, peeled, cored and finely chopped

350g (14oz) raisins

225g (9oz) sultanas

225g (9oz) currants

100g (4oz) mixed peel, finely chopped

100g (4oz) natural glacé cherries

Grated zest and juice of 2 oranges

Grated zest and juice of 2 lemons

4 teaspoons ground mixed spice

½ teaspoon ground nutmeg

½ teaspoon allspice

350g (14oz) soft dark brown sugar

50g (2oz) whole almonds, cut into slivers

6 tablespoons brandy

For the mince pies

1 quantity of sweet pastry (p. 30)

1 beaten egg

Icing sugar to decorate

Mincemeat

Prepare this well in advance of making mince pies. The mincemeat will keep for six months.

Preheat the oven to Gas Mark 6/200°C/400°F.

Wash 6 x 1lb (450g) jam jars in warm soapy water. Then place in a preheated oven for 1 hour to dry and sterilise them.

Melt the butter/margarine.

Mix the apple, dried fruit, zest, spices, brown sugar and almonds together in a large bowl, very thoroughly.

Add the butter/margarine, fruit juices and brandy and stir well.

Cover with a cloth and leave for 12 hours to mature.

Spoon into the clean dry jars with screw top lids.

This will mature in the jar and store for 6 months.

Mince pies

Make the pastry according to the instructions.

Preheat the oven to Gas Mark 6/200°C/400°F. Line a twelve-hole queen cake tin with paper cases.

Roll out the pastry on a board floured with a little potato flour. Use a small scone cutter to cut circles and fit to the paper cases. Cut out a matching lid for each pie. Alternatively, using a small star-shaped cookie cutter, cut out a festive-shaped top for the mince pies and use the star instead of a lid, as I have done in the photo.

Fill the pastry cups with the mincemeat (not too much – only to the level of the edges of the pastry).

Now dampen the edges of the pastry lids with water and press them lightly into position, sealing the edges. Brush each one with beaten egg and make about three snips into the top with a pair of scissors to make air holes. If using a festive-shaped top, just press this firmly onto the middle of each mince pie and brush with beaten egg.

Bake in the centre of the oven for 25–30 minutes until golden brown. Then remove gently from the trays and paper cases and cool them on a wire tray. Sprinkle with sieved icing sugar. Store the cooled mince pies in an airtight tin and warm them slightly before serving.

Mum's traditional Christmas trifle with crème pâtissière

Everybody loves trifle. It's a special occasion dish that requires a bit of patience as each layer sets in the fridge, but it's always worth it!

Sponge base

100g (4oz) Denise's Delicious flour blend (p. 28) · 1 teaspoon GF baking powder

½ teaspoon xanthan gum · 50g (2oz) butter/margarine, at room temperature

2 large eggs · 100g (4oz) caster sugar, plus a little extra

1 teaspoon vanilla extract

To assemble

2–3 tablespoons raspberry jam · 150ml (5floz) rich Madeira

2 packets raspberry jelly · 2 bananas · Juice of ½ lemon

Crème pâtissière

6 medium egg yolks · 115g (4½oz) caster sugar · 40g (1½oz) corn flour

510ml (17floz) milk · 1 vanilla pod, split · Icing sugar, to dust

To finish

270ml (9floz) double cream

50g (2oz) flaked almonds, lightly toasted

Sponge base

You can prepare the sponge the day before serving if it is convenient. Preheat the oven to Gas Mark 5/190°C/375°F. Grease a 25cm x 30cm/10in x12in Swiss roll tin and line it with baking parchment.

Sieve the flour, baking powder and gum together.

In a separate bowl, place the butter/margarine, eggs, caster sugar and vanilla extract and, using an electric mixture, mix for about a minute to a smooth creamy consistency. Then add the flour and combine fully, using the mixer on a low setting.

Spread the mixture evenly in the prepared tin. Don't worry if it looks a bit sparse because it will increase in size.

Bake in the centre of the oven for 14–20 minutes or until it is golden brown and a skewer comes out dry.

To assemble

When the sponge is cool, cover with raspberry jam and cut into fingers. Next, arrange the pieces in the base of a large trifle/dessert bowl or four large wine glasses and drizzle the Madeira all over them as evenly as possible.

Make a packet of raspberry jelly and when cooled but not set, pour over the sponge. Put in the fridge overnight to set.

The following day, make another packet of raspberry jelly and set aside to cool. Slice the bananas quite thinly and mix with the lemon juice (this will prevent them from discolouring). Sprinkle them over the set jelly in the trifle bowl/glasses and then pour on the cooled jelly. The bananas will float to the top. Return to the fridge to set.

Crème pâtissière

Place the egg yolks and about one-third of the sugar in a bowl and whisk until pale and forming a light ribbon when the whisk is lifted out of the mixture.

Sieve the corn flour and mix well into the egg mixture.

Combine the milk, the remaining sugar and the split vanilla pod in a saucepan and bring to the boil. As soon as the mixture bubbles, pour about one-third onto the egg mixture, whisking vigorously all the time.

Remove the vanilla pod, then scrape out the vanilla seeds and add the seeds to the egg mixture.

Pour the mixture back into the pan with the rest of the milk and cook over a gentle heat, whisking continuously. Boil for 2 minutes, then pour the crème pâtissière into a bowl. Sprinkle with icing sugar and cover with a circle of greaseproof paper, to stop a skin forming, and leave to cool.

When the jelly has set, pour the crème pâtissière over it and place in the fridge again.

To finish

Whip the double cream with an electric hand-held whisk until it is firm but still soft. Spread the cream over the top and scatter with flaked almonds that have been lightly toasted under the grill.

Cover with cling film and store in the fridge until ready to serve.

Festive Yule log with rum

There's something so Christmassy about a Yule log. For me, Christmas is not complete without it. You can always add a little extra rum if you are so inclined!

25g (1oz) cocoa powder

100g (4oz) Denise's Delicious flour blend (p. 28)

1 level teaspoon GF baking powder

½ teaspoon xanthan gum

50g (2oz) butter/margarine, at room temperature

2 large eggs

100g (4oz) caster sugar, plus a little extra

1 teaspoon vanilla extract

Icing sugar to dust

Filling

200g (8oz) icing sugar

25g (1oz) cocoa powder

75g (3oz) butter/margarine at room temperature, cubed

3 teaspoons rum

Preheat the oven to Gas Mark 5/190°C/375°F. Grease a 25cm x 30cm/10in x 12in Swiss roll tin and line it with baking parchment.

Sieve the cocoa and then sieve the flour, baking powder, gum and cocoa powder together three times to get rid of any lumps in the cocoa and to blend it properly.

In a separate bowl, mix the butter/margarine, eggs, caster sugar and vanilla extract to a smooth creamy consistency using an electric mixer, for about a minute. Then add the flour and cocoa mixture and combine fully, using the mixer on a low setting.

Spread the mixture evenly in the prepared tin, smoothing it with the back of a tablespoon. Do not worry if it looks a bit sparse because it will increase in size.

Bake the Swiss roll in the centre of the oven for 20–25 minutes until golden brown and a skewer inserted in the centre comes out dry.

While it is baking you can prepare everything for the rolling operation. First of all you need a damp tea towel spread out on a flat surface (and a second one ready for later), then on top of the tea towel place a sheet of baking parchment that is about 2½cm/1in larger than the tin. Sprinkle caster sugar all over the paper.

As soon as the Swiss roll is baked, remove from the oven and, holding the sides of the lining, turn it out onto the prepared baking parchment.

Now carefully and gently strip off the liner, take a sharp knife and trim 3mm/⅛in from all round the cake. This will make it much neater and help to prevent it from cracking.

Cover with a clean, damp tea towel and leave for a

couple of minutes. Then, with one of the shorter edges of the cake nearest to you, make a small incision about 2½cm from the edge, cutting right across the cake but not too deeply; this will help you when you start to roll.

Now start by rolling this 2½cm/1in piece over and away from you and continue to roll, using the sugared paper to help you roll the whole thing up by pulling it up behind the cake as it rolls.

Filling

Sieve the icing sugar and cocoa powder together three times to combine fully and remove all the lumps.

Add the cubed butter to the icing sugar in a medium-sized mixing bowl and combine using an electric mixer on a low speed.

Once it has mixed, add the rum, increase the speed to medium and beat well.

The consistency you are aiming for is fluffy and smooth – make sure there are no lumps of margarine or cocoa.

Gently unroll the Swiss roll. It will not unroll fully and do not force it. A pallet knife will allow you to tuck the buttercream into the corners that are not fully unrolled.

Smooth half of the buttercream icing onto the inside of the Swiss roll with a pallet knife. For this to be problem free, ensure that the buttercream is at room temperature. If it is cold it becomes very stiff and is difficult to spread.

Have a bowl of warm water to hand and dip the pallet knife into this between each application of buttercream. It will help to spread the buttercream more easily.

Now, roll up the Swiss roll again and then smooth the remaining buttercream on to the outside and ends of the Swiss roll. Be careful not to tear the sponge.

Place on a festive plate and dust with sieved icing sugar to resemble snow and place a sprig of holly and a robin decoration on top.

Index

Notes

Notes

Notes

Denise's Delicious

GLUTEN FREE BAKERY

If you would like to find out more about
Denise's Delicious Gluten Free Bakery, or
order through her online shop, you can get
in touch using the details below:

W: www.delicious.ie
E: denise@delicious.ie

Unit 17/18 Euro Innovation Business Park
Little Island
Cork
Ireland